One Minute Mandarin

One Minute Mandarin
A beginner's guide to spoken Chinese for professionals

Peter Coyne

ALLEN&UNWIN

Material from *The Analects of Confucius*, translated by Simon Leys.
Copyright © 1997 by Pierre Ryckmans. Used by permission of W. W.
Norton & Company, Inc.

First published in 2008

Copyright © Peter Coyne 2008

Allen & Unwin
83 Alexander Street
Crows Nest NSW 2065
Australia
Phone: (61 2) 8425 0100
Fax: (61 2) 9906 2218
Email: info@allenandunwin.com
Web: www.allenandunwin.com

National Library of Australia
Cataloguing-in-Publication entry:

Coyne, Peter.

 One minute Mandarin : a beginner's guide to spoken Chinese
 for professionals / author, Peter Coyne.

 Crows Nest, N.S.W. : Allen & Unwin, 2008.

 978 1 74175 459 9 (pbk.) :

 Mandarin dialects - Conversation and phrase books (for
 professionals) - English. Chinese language - Conversation
 and phrase books (for professionals) - English. Chinese
 language - Business Chinese.

495.182421

Set in 11/14.5 pt Warnock Pro by Bookhouse, Sydney

To A.E.V.
who showed that it could be done

This book is accompanied by a website with downloadable mp3 files for your iPod, mp3 player, PC or laptop. The clips feature spoken examples of key sounds, words and phrases which you can use to tune in your ear to correct Mandarin pronunciation.

See www.allenandunwin.com/mandarin

Contents

Introduction

He who does not understand words is incapable of understanding men

The Analects of Confucius, 20.3 (Leys trans.)

The idea for this book stemmed from my experience teaching Chinese to very busy people. My students have included corporate CEOs and a cabinet minister and I quickly became aware of the need to tailor language material to meet practical needs within limited timeframes created by professional commitments. These people did not expect to become fluent in conversation but wanted to acquire enough usable language that reflected their interest and which could help establish some ready rapport with their counterparts in China. Such beginners with a firm view on practical needs often comment 'I just want to be able to say...'. My own experience of learning and using Chinese over many years taught me that a number of highly useful expressions can be easily learned and are adaptable to a variety of social situations. Most importantly they establish a connection with native speakers and through them an appreciation of the cultural context of the Chinese language.

This introduction to spoken Mandarin Chinese for the adult learner uses practical methods to deal with the mismatch between ability and needs. The selection of words and phrases is based on their usefulness in more sophisticated social situations while recognizing the need for ease of learning and pronunciation. The introduction to the usages of different words and phrases have been carefully selected to avoid overly complex grammar while still being able to be used as stand alone comments in appropriate situations.

It is possible to learn sufficient and useful Chinese with a minimum but sustained effort without learning the Chinese script. The approach of this book makes great use of the limited sound structure and economy of expression that characterise the Chinese language. The use of the pinyin spelling system, the official romanisation system in China, can be quickly mastered as a tool for progressing learning. With the veil of the Chinese characters removed the elegant simplicity of both Chinese grammar as well as the sound system is revealed. Like many things Chinese, there is a premium on the use of flexibility and adaptability which in terms of language means that a little can go a long way—great news for users of this book!

The simplicity and economy of the Mandarin sound system mean that the basics of pronunciation can be quickly learned. A detailed pronounciation guide, with a note on tones, features at the start of this book. It is recommended that you reveiw this before delving into the chapters. To assist familiarization with the spelling system, within the chapters pronunciation is provided in square brackets to aid memory.

While tones are important it is not necessary to get the tone right first time—most Chinese speakers bring their regional accents to Mandarin which even in the case of northern speakers can mean some heavy accents. Tones and pronunciation will improve with familiarity and use.

The inclusion of proverbial sayings in this book acknowledges their important place in ordinary speech as well as the extent to which such proverbs reflect much of the charm and spirit of the language. It has been observed that 'the Chinese perhaps more than any other people are world-renowned for their proverbs, and proverbs have long played and continue to play an important role in both their oral and written traditions up to the present day' (Rohsenow, *ABC Dictionary of Chinese Proverbs*, xvii). Short proverbial sayings are structured for oral memorization and can be used for maximum effect as stand alone expressions without the need for more complex linguistic support. Very common sayings have been selected for their relative ease of pronunciation. They can be used effectively from the earliest engagement with the language to the delighted surprise of listeners. The continued use of proverbial language in Chinese reflects an educational tradition that has always placed a premium on oral repetition and rote memorization. More importantly, proverbs express traditional knowledge and values that still resonate with speakers today.

How this book works

This practical introduction to spoken Mandarin Chinese is structured around a number of sentences and expressions that can be immediately used. The vocabulary and grammar of each key expression is explained together with further examples of related usages. Where appropriate, linguistic and cultural notes are provided for additional background. The order of the key expressions has been arranged according to likely social situations that will confront the adult visitor to China whether on an official visit or for pleasure. The basic language patterns and grammatical structures introduced provide a useful foundation for further, more formal, study. The selection covers a large proportion of Chinese grammatical structures and patterns.

This guide can also be productively used by a native-speaker tutor. While the content is designed to be suitable for self-study, access to an experienced (native or foreign) speaker to correct pronunciation and intonation is recommended. Few native speakers of any language are equipped to teach their own language, though appropriate teaching material can make the most productive use of both the student and teacher's time. Most native speakers are unaware of the language needs of the adult foreign learner as well as the shortcuts in their language that have been (arduously) acquired by fluent foreign speakers.

The accompanying MP3 pronunciation guide contains the main sentence patterns as well as vocabulary provided in the text. It is recommended that you listen to each lesson a couple of times to become familiar with the sound patterns. Pronounce each sound as naturally as you can without straining for perfect accuracy. The examples are very basic vocabulary that is easily understood. Remember that context is all and for native Chinese speakers also it is most often the sounds around each word that communicate meaning rather than individual sounds. Familiarity will come with practice.

It hardly needs saying that communication is about much more than language, even so there remains few more convenient bridges into another culture than the spoken word. Confucius himself appreciated this point when he said: 'He who does not understand words is incapable of understanding men.' In its practical guidance to matters of social intercourse this principle underpins much of the content that provides some background to the cultural milieu of the people that use the language.

A modest aim of this work is that it will stimulate further interest in both the language and culture of China. An indication of interest usually meets with appreciation and respect for foreigners who have gone to the trouble to acquaint themselves, no matter how rudimentarily, with the Chinese language. If this occurs even occasionally the purpose of this guide can be considered to have been realized. Enjoy!

Note on sounds in Chinese

Chinese words are usually created by two Chinese characters and it is useful to remember that each individual Chinese word sound is composed of two syllables—an initial and a final sound syllable. *Together* they produce a *single* sound. Chinese is characterized by an extremely limited number of basic sounds. The finite number of sound units are increased by the use of tones. (For more detail on pronunication and tones see the next section). It is important to pronounce the sound syllables as a single unit, not as separate sounds. For example, n+ee = ni, N+an = nan; Ni+an = nian [pronounced 'nyan']. Please note that in this book pronunciation is provided in brackets as a guide and aide memoire only and is not exact.

Chinese Pronunciation
A guide to pinyin spelling

Chinese pronunciation is difficult in so far as few sounds correspond exactly with those in English, but it can be mastered very quickly once the basic principles of the sound system are understood. There are only four tones and just over four hundred single syllables that are used to produce the actual twelve hundred sound patterns of syllable groups forming words that are used in Mandarin. Emphasis should be given to getting the *pronunciation* of the sounds as correct as possible. Tonal patterns should then follow.

Initial sounds (that are not intuitive):

q	<u>ch</u>ew
x	<u>sh</u>e
zh	Geor<u>ge</u>
c	i<u>ts</u>

Consonants and vowels used alone or in final syllables:

a	ah	*ai*	eye
ia	yar	*uai*	Ha<u>wai</u>i
ua	wah	*ei*	m<u>ay</u>
o	w<u>ar</u>; t<u>all</u>	*uei*	oo-ay
uo	l<u>oo</u>k + or	*ao*	h<u>ow</u>
e	<u>ear</u>ly	*iao*	ee-ow
ie	<u>ye</u>s	*üe*	you-eh
ou	oh	*iou*	ee-o
an	<u>un</u>der	*ian*	yen
üan	you-an	*en*	brok<u>en</u>
in	inn	*ün*	oo-n
ang	h<u>ung</u>	*iang*	ee-ung
eng	<u>ng</u>	*ing*	s<u>ing</u>
ueng	oo-ng	*uang*	oo-ung
ong	b<u>oo</u>k-ng	*iong*	ee-oo-ng

It is important to bear in mind that the standard forms of pronunciation will be encountered more often among educated speakers in the major cities. It is very common to hear standard Chinese spoken with regional accents and pronunciation is the most obvious way of establishing people's regional origins. For example, a major feature of northern pronunciation is the tendency to end words with the 'r' sound which is produced by curling the tongue back in the mouth. This ability is the most obvious pronunciation feature distinguishing northern and southern speakers. Hence with Southerners the 'shr' sound is produced more like 'see'. Similarly, any sound that requires this tongue position (e.g. chi, zhi) will be flattened and produced with the tongue close to the front of the mouth to sound like the sound 'z'. Foreign speakers are frequently complimented on their accurate pronunciation—usually by speakers with strong regional accents.

Tones in Chinese

Tones are most easily understood as the particular stress or emphasis on any individual syllable. In Chinese, such stress can produce a word with a different meaning. This use of stress is not foreign to the English speaker and is frequently used, for example:

> You did <u>what</u>?
> <u>Who</u> said you could go?
> Just <u>do</u> it.
> That doesn't mean a <u>thing</u>.
> That's <u>strange</u>.

Stress in Chinese works in a similar but much more controlled way. Standard Mandarin has four tones:

- An even (first) tone indicated in the text by ˉ . The tone is flat, high and does not change pitch.
- A rising (second) tone indicated by ´ is slightly longer in its sound than a first tone and has a rising pitch. Think of 'who' in the above example.
- A falling and rising (third) tone indicated by ˇ begins with a slightly deeper pitch before rising. It has the longest sound. Think of 'strange'.

- The fourth tone indicated by ˋ is a short sharp declining pitch. Think of 'thing' and 'do' in the above examples.

For example the single syllable *ma* pronounced in the first tone means 'mother', in the second tone *ma* means 'hemp', in the third tone it means 'horse' and the fourth tone 'to curse'.

While tones are important try not to worry about them too much in the beginning—they are not critical to mutual comprehension. Context is all. Mastery of tones comes with some practice. In fluent speech the overall tonal pattern of the sentence is more important than the tones of the individual syllables.

It is also important to be aware that not all words have stressed tones or some lose their stress when added to another which is emphasized and becomes longer. Also, tones change regularly in two particular circumstances—a third tone followed immediately by another third tone will change to a second (rising) tone, for example, *ní hǎo*; a fourth tone followed immediately by another fourth tone will be pronounced as a rising second tone, for example *bú yào*. You will find that these changes come quite naturally after time and make pronunciation easier. Of course there are always exceptions to this, one being when words are spoken with added emphasis they are given their original tones. In this book the modifications of the tonal patterns as actually spoken are what largely appear (not those that appear in the dictionary) though foreign words are an exception.

1

How do you do Mr Wang?
Ní hǎo Wáng xiān sheng?

nǐ [n + be̲] *you; 2ⁿᵈ personal singular*
hǎo [how] *good; well; fine; OK*
ní hǎo (lit. you good) *hello; how are you; how do you do?*

This is the most common form of greeting in China today. It can also be used as the response. You should be aware that this is an instance of one of the most common tone changes—where two third tones appear together the first becomes a second tone with no change to the meaning. Many examples follow. You can say:

Ní hǎo ma?

Ma is unstressed; similar to the unstressed first syllable in m̲ature. Used at the end of a sentence this is one of the most common ways to create a question. *Ma* is one of a number of sound particles used in Chinese that have no inherent meaning by themselves. For example you can say:

Hǎo ma? *OK? All right?; Shall we?*

By adding the particle *men* [m + op<u>en</u>] you create a plural, such as *nǐ men*. Note that this syllable is unstressed. *Men* is one of the few language particles in Chinese that cannot be used alone. It can only be added to certain nouns referring to persons when no definite number is mentioned, for example:

péng [<u>up</u> + si<u>ng</u>] *you* [yoh] *men*   friends
tóng [toong] *zhì* [jr] *men*   comrades

A polite version of *nǐ* is *nín*. This may be used by a guest to a host or when addressing someone older or in a position of authority to show respect. This form of address may be used by you as a visitor or guest, as in *nín hǎo ma*. In China today this polite usage has re-emerged.

Cultural note

In modern China the word 'comrade' is increasingly used as a humourous anachronism, though still used in its strict meaning between Communist Party members. Now possibly more commonly heard among homosexuals to mean 'gay'.

A general response to *Nǐ hǎo ma?* can be:

Hěn hǎo xiè xie   Very well, thank you.
   hěn [h + op<u>en</u>]   *very; quite*. Always precedes an adjective. It is slightly weaker than 'very' in English and often does not add much to the meaning.
   xiè xie [She + yeh as one syllable sounds a little like the English 'share']   *thank you*. The second syllable is unstressed.

Xiè xie is an example of a word which is devised of a repetition of one sound. This is a feature of the Chinese language. Many examples are given in this book.

Cultural note

Xiè xie is used as an expression of appreciation or gratitude for what has been said. It is important to keep in mind it does not mean 'yes!' or express agreement. *Xiè xie* is a polite way to resond without making a commitment to act on what has been said!

Related Expressions

Qiān xiè wàn xiè   *I cannot thank you enough!* (lit. a thousand thanks)
   qiān [chi + <u>any</u>]   *one thousand*
   wàn [one]   *ten thousand*

Wéi [w + m<u>ay</u>]   *hello; hey there!* (Used on the telephone or to attract someone's attention.)

Nǐ zhēn hǎo   *How good of you; You're really good.*
   zhēn [djen]   *true; real*

Hǎo jí le   *That's delightful; I'd be delighted.*
   Jí [gee] *le* (l + h<u>er</u>) Used to register an extreme and can be used after many adjectives.

Wáng [w + h<u>ung</u>] This is a common surname, often rendered in English as Wong. It is a small but appreciated courtesy to pronounce correctly the name of the person you are speaking to (A full list of common surnames is at Appendix A).

Note that there is a general preference in Chinese for an order of precedence to be established and what is considered the most important will be expressed first. In the case of *Ní hǎo Wáng xiān sheng* the surname precedes the title. While there are many similar examples at the purely linguistic level it is useful to keep this in mind as a general expression of Chinese pragmatism—first things first! In keeping with this principle the above sentence can also be expressed as:

> *Wáng xiān sheng ní hǎo ma?*
> *xiān* [see + <u>any</u>] *sheng* [sh + h<u>er</u> + si<u>ng</u>]   *Mr; sir* (lit. first born).

It is used in direct address to follow surnames. This can be used to mean 'gentleman' or 'my husband'. Note that *sheng* is unstressed here. The plural is:

> *Xiān sheng men*   gentlemen (plural)

You may hear the term *xiān sheng* used very occasionally as a title referring to a woman in which case it is an extremely respectful term for a distinguished person, for example, a university professor.

Cultural note

It is preferable to use titles rather than names, where possible, as a sign of courtesy. In a status-conscious society if someone has a title, not only will they like to be reminded of it, but they will also be pleased that you are aware of it. This applies particularly to people in senior positions (e.g. directors; chairmen; government ministers; teachers etc.) Use of the third person may be preferable to use rather than the informal 'you'. Any title will usually be provided on a name card. It is worth taking the time to get the title right and use it correctly as a mark of respect. Note that there is no easy equivalent of **xiān sheng** for women and an official title is usually preferable to the equivalent of Miss/Mrs/Madame etc. A list of commonly encountered titles can be found in Appendix A.

In general terms formality is associated with being polite. When in doubt be courteous! Profuse thanks for the smallest gesture will never be considered out of place. A common saying has it that *lǐ duō rén bù guài* (lit. manners many people not [think] strange), meaning that no one will blame you for excessive courtesy—you cannot be too polite.

Proverb

súi xīn sǔo yù

Follow your heart; do as you please.

súi	follow
xīn	heart
sǔo	that
yù	desire, wish

A quote from Confucius (551–479 BC) that is part of his account of his gradual progress and attainment of wisdom. The full quote puts this into context:

At fifteen, I set my mind on learning.
At thirty, I took my stand.
At forty, I had no doubts.
At fifty, I knew the will of Heaven.
At sixty, my ear was attuned.
At seventy, I follow all the desires of my heart without breaking any rules. (*Analects:* 2.4.; Leys trans.)

The Analects comprise of responses Confucius provided to his 72 disciples who toured the countryside with him during the turbulent times of the Warring States period. Originally reviled by the Communist Party and progressive thinkers, the reputation of China's foremost sage has undergone a remarkable revival in recent years and his works that articulate a secular humanist ethical tradition are at the forefront of a popular resurgence of interest in China's classical literary heritage. Modern editions of this venerable text are widely available in most bookshops and a recent commentary from a television lecture series is said to have sold some four million copies in China.

2

I am very happy to meet you
Wó hĕn gāo xìng jiàn dào nǐ

wŏ [war]   *I; me; first person singular*

As noted in Chapter 1 *men* may be added to create the plural: *wŏ men*   *we*

Wŏ ma?   *(who) me?*

gāo [gow] *xìng* [shing]   *be happy; delighted; elated*

Chinese adjectives include the verbs 'to be', so this expression means 'to be happy'. Hence you may ask the question:

Q: *Nĭ gāo xìng ma?*   *Are you happy/pleased?*

A: *Hĕn gāo xìng*   *I am very pleased/happy.*

Gāo used by itself is an adjective that means to be tall or high. You can say:

Tā hĕn gāo   *He is (very) tall.*

Jiàn [gee + <u>any</u>]   *to see; to meet*

This sound appears in the phrase:

> **Zài jiàn** *goodbye; see you again*
>   *zài* [it<u>s</u> + eye] *again*

> **dào** [dow] *to arrive* (at); *to reach; get to* (a place)

The word is used here to indicate the result of an action, for example, 'the result of my seeing (you) is that I am happy'. In its original meaning this word can be used in expressions like:

> **Wǒ men dào le** *We have arrived; we're here.*
> **Dào le ma?** *Are we there yet?*

The unstressed particle *le* is widely used to indicate a completed action. It can also be used to indicate that a change of circumstances has taken place. Listen out for it; its usage remains one of the most difficult in the language to master!

The possessive

The possessive is created by using the particle: *de* [h<u>e</u>r]; the sound in this usage is unstressed.

> **Wǒ de** *my; mine*
> **Wǒ men de** *our; ours*
> **Nǐ de** *your; yours*
> **Nǐ men de** *you* (plural); *yours*
> **Wǒ de ma?** *Is it for me; is it mine?*
> **Nǐ de ma?** *Is this yours?*

Note that the *de* is sometimes dropped, especially after plurals.

Grammar note

In Chinese, nouns as well as verbs do not take endings to indicate plural or tense (*men* used to form the plural of words denoting persons being the exception). Words can be considered as building blocks that can be moved around to create sentences that overall conform to the subject-verb-object word order as in English. The context will usually (but not always) determine the subject and tense of the verb. This permits much flexibility as well as ambiguity—that may be used intentionally! It is also important to bear in mind that subjects may not be overtly expressed.

As subjects (and objects) may be omitted where they are understood, sentence structures in spoken Chinese can be greatly simplified. It is another display of the Chinese genius for economy and filtering out what is considered extraneous. Therefore the Chinese language is very good at cutting to the chase in communication or avoiding a subject entirely, which might be the prerogative of the speaker and something to which an attentive listener is attuned.

Another useful expression when meeting someone involves the use of:

Yuán [you + Anne]   *affinity; connection; reason*

Yuán fèn [orphan]   *a providential opportunity;* fate/luck
by which people are brought together
Wǒ men yǒu yuán fèn   *we were fated to meet*

Yuán is also used in such words as: *yuán gù:* cause; reason; *yuán yóu: cause; origin*

A popular saying has it that if people are fated to meet they will, no matter how far apart and if not they will miss each other even though they come face to face. This use of *yuán* in this expression reflects the enduring presence of Buddhism (*fó jiào*) [for + gee + c<u>ow</u>] in Chinese life. *Yuán* is used to express the Buddhist concept of karma.

Cultural note

Buddhism first entered China with monks from India sometime in the first century AD and quickly began to acquire distinctly Chinese characteristics (e.g. Chinese monks could marry). It emerged as a singular and enduring influence on thought, the arts and social life, joining Confucianism and Daoism to become one of the three classic religions of China. Buddhism has re-established its position at the centre of religious belief and practice in China after near total suppression during the Cultural Revolution (1966–1976). *Ē mí tuó fó* or *ná mò ē mí tuó fó* (lit. Amida Buddha is merciful) is a commonly used expression of both greeting and thanks among Buddhist believers—lay as well as religious.

Proverb

Yŏu zhì jìng chéng

Where there's a will there's a way.

yŏu	have
zhì	will
jìng	in the end
chéng	succeed

Attributed to the famous general Geng Yan (3–58 AD) when praised by the emperor for his victory over rebels, though his army was greatly outnumbered, during the chaotic period of the consolidation of the Eastern Han dynasty (25–220 AD). The historical context of the original saying is a reminder of the geographical division that was often a part of China's tumultuous past.

3

Welcome to China!

Huān yíng nǐ lái zhōng guó

huān [hwan] *yíng* [yet + s<u>ing</u>]   *welcome*

Can be used alone with this meaning but also often used in repetition as: *huān yíng huān yíng*

The word *lái* [lie], meaning 'to come' may be used in the following ways:

> *Wǒ lái le*   *I am coming; I am on my way.*
> *Nǐ lái ma?*   *Are you coming?*
> *zài* [<u>its</u> + eye] *lái*   *come again; another...(e.g. I'd like another beer.)*

> *Zhōng Guó* is the Mandarin term for China:
> *zhōng* [djoong—oo as in c<u>oo</u>k]   *middle*
> *guó* [gwor]   *country*

Gúo can be used as a suffix to create a number of country names:

> *Měi* [may] *guó*   *the United States of America*
> *Yīng guó*   *the United Kingdom*

Fǎ [fah] *guó*   France
Dé [der] *guó*   Germany

Appendix B includes a list of more country names.

The complementary verb is *qù* [chew] meaning 'to go'. This may be used as follows:

Nǐ qù ma?   *Are you going?*
Wǒ qù le   *I went* (there)
Nǐ qù zhōng guó ma?   *Are you going to China?*

Useful expressions of welcome:

Huān yíng nǐ lái wǒ men   *Welcome to our:*
   gōng [cook] *sī* [mass]   *company* (as in business)
   chéng [ch + her + ng] *shì* [shr]   *city*
   gōng chǎng [ch + hung]   *factory*
   shǒu [show] *dū* [do]   *capital city*
   jiā [gee + ah]   *home*

Wǒ hěn gāo xìng lái zhōng guó   *I am very happy to be in China.*

There may often be occasions when you may wish to be more effusive in thanking someone for some action. The following may be used:

Tài [tie] *xiè xie nǐ le*   *thank you very much*
   tài   *too; extremely.* Used before most verbs and adjectives.

Fēi [fay] *cháng* [ch + h<u>ung</u>] *xiè xie*   *thank you very much*
   fēi cháng   *very; extremely; highly.* This word has the
      original meaning of extraordinary or unusual and
      can be used before adjectives to express exceptional
      degree.

Wǒ fēi cháng gāo xìng   *I am extremely happy.*

Cultural note

Expressing gratitude and thanks is an extremely important aspect of courtesy as 'one who does not repay a debt of gratitude is not a gentleman'. Another popular saying recalls that 'when drinking water do not forget those who dug the well (*chī shuǐ bú wàng jué jǐng rén*); in other words, do not be ungrateful to those who have helped you in the past. Though it is just as well to remember that less positive sentiments also have a long shelf life, as another popular saying has it, 'gratitude as well as hatred do not diminish with time'.

Proverb

Wàng měi zhí kě

Console oneself with false hopes;
feed on fancies.

wàng	look
měi	plum
zhí	stop
kě	thirsty

A strategem attributed to the famous general Cao Cao (d. 220 AD) who was one of the most prominent figures to appear during the time of the disintegration of the Han dynasty into the period of the Three Kingdoms (220–265 AD). On one occasion he is said to have urged his distressed army on during the heat of summer by telling them of plum trees up ahead. The thought of the plums was sufficient to produce thirst quenching saliva in the soldiers' mouths that enabled them to continue the march through arid countryside. The expression describes consoling oneself with imaginary thoughts in the face of a hope that cannot be achieved.

4

Long time no see!

Háo jiŭ bú jiàn

This phrase means just what it says (lit. 'long time no see') and can be used when meeting again after a long separation, just as we do in English.

jiŭ [gee + you]   *be long* (referring to time)

To ask 'How long?' (referring to time) use the expression:

Duō [door] *jiŭ?*   *How long will it/does it take?*

Related expressions

hěn duō   *very many; very much*

Nĭ lái zhōng guó duō jiŭ?   *How long have you been in China?*

Nĭ lái (le) duō jiŭ?   *How long have you been here?*

Jiú yǎng jiú yǎng   *It's a pleasure to meet you (at last).* This is a more formal expression that draws on the classical language.

Negatives

Bù [book]   *not; no*

This is one of the most important words used to say 'no' as well as make a negative. It always appears directly before the word it negates which can be a verb, adjective or adverb. Note that **bù** will change to a second tone when in front of another fourth tone. It can be used as follows:

Bù, bù bù   *no, no, no!* (for emphasis)
Q: *Hǎo ma?*   *OK?*
A: *Bù hǎo*   *It's no/not good; not OK*
Tā bù gāo xìng   *He is not pleased/happy*
Nǐ bù gāo xìng ma?   *Aren't you pleased/happy?*
Wǒ bù lái   *I am not coming*
Nǐ bù lái ma?   *Aren't you coming? Won't you come?*
Nǐ bú qù ma?   *Aren't you going?*

A very useful example of this construction is *hǎo bù hǎo* which is used to create the expression to solicit agreement, as in 'do you think this is OK or not?'. This can be used as a stand-alone expression in relation to any situation where an opinion is sought because you can use it like you would use 'May I?' or 'Shall we?'.

Similar expressions using this construction to form questions (as an alternative to using *ma* at the end of a sentence) are:

Qù bú qù?   *Are you going or not?*
Lái bù lái?   *Are you coming or not?*

Gāo xìng bù gāo xìng? (Are you/is he) *happy or not?*
Wǒ men qù hǎo bù hǎo? Shall we go? Do you feel like going?

The other most important expression of the negative (and one that you may hear much more often than you would like) is: *méi* [may] which means 'do not have' or 'do not possess' and may be commonly used as follows:

méi yǒu [yoh] *there is no; we have no*
yǒu to have; possess; there is/are/were
Nǐ yǒu ma? Do you have it/any?
Nǐ yǒu méi yǒu? Do you have it/any?

As a stand alone expression it has a wide variety of contextual meanings such as 'no' to negate a verb (see below); I/we do not have it/any; it is off the menu/out of stock/sold out.

It may be used as:

Wǒ méi yǒu I do not have it; I have never (done something); *I don't* (depending on context)

It may also be used before certain verbs as a past negative:

Tā méi lái He did not come; he has not come yet
Nǐ méi qù ma? You didn't go? You haven't been?
Méi yǒu yuán (fèn) That was not meant (fated) to happen.

Other useful expressions with *méi*:

hái [hi] *méi yǒu not yet* (of an action or situation)

Hái méi yǒu lái   (He) *has not come yet*

Méi (yǒu) guān [g + one] *xi* [shee]   *it doesn't matter; it is unimportant; think nothing of it; it is not relevant.*

Guān xi   *connection; relationship*

Tā guān xi hén hǎo   *he is well connected; he is on good terms (with...); he's influential* (*xi* is unstressed here)

Yǒu guān xi ma?   *is it related; relevant?*

Other common expressions with *méi* (*yǒu* is often omitted):

(Wo) *méi bàn* [bun] *fǎ* [fah]   *I'm at a loss; stymied*
   bàn fǎ   *method; way; means; solution*

bàn fǎ can be used positively in the following:

   Tā hén yǒu bàn fǎ   *He is very capable.*
   Ní yǒu bàn fǎ ma?   *Can you manage?*
Méi shénma [shemma]   *That's all right; You're welcome* (e.g. in response to *xiè xie.*)

méi shì is a very useful expression as it can be used in response to an apology to mean 'it doesn't matter' or 'never mind' and can also be a response to *xiè xie* (thank you) as in 'it's all right'. The phrase *wǒ méi shì* means to have nothing to do (i.e. to be free) as in 'I'm not busy'.

It also occurs in the expression:
   méi shì zhǎo [george + cow] *shì*   (lit. look for trouble).

Yǒu and *méi yǒu* may be counted among the most useful words to know how to use.

Cultural note

Guān xi is an often untranslated expression that gives the impression it is a uniquely Chinese concept. It has become the subject of some considerable study by China scholars as a key term in understanding the dynamics of social relationships in China. Understood as relationship, networks or connections it is not a term difficult to understand. By extension, the word has the meaning of influence, bearing (on a matter) and significance. Like any society China can be understood as a network of connections consisting of family ties, education and work associations that can be crucially important in getting things done. Friendships that establish *guān xi* are very useful in cutting through red tape and gaining preferential treatment.

Proverb

Sài wēng shī mǎ
A blessing in disguise.

sài	a frontier border
wēng	old man
shī	lose
mǎ	horse

This proverb literally means 'the old man on the frontier lost his horse' and refers to a popular fable that tells of an old man living at the northern border with his son who loved riding. Though one of his horses ran off and was lost he remained unconcerned and it ended up returning with another fine steed. The son tried to ride the horse but fell off and broke his leg. This apparent misfortune was soon followed by an outbreak of war along the frontier, and because of his injury the old man's son was able to avoid military service. The second line of the proverb is ***ān zhī fēi fú*** (i.e. who could have known it was a blessing?). The saying is used to mean that a loss may turn out to be a gain.

The proverb is based on a popular fable that appeared in the *Huai nan zi*, (dated from the 2nd century BC) a collection of essays largely Daoist in inspiration that is one of the most important philosophical works of the early Han dynasty, and represents a synthesis of earlier thought.

5

He/she is Chinese
Tā shì zhōng guó rén

tā [tah]   *he/she/it*

The plural is:

tā men   *they; them*
tā men dào le ma?   *Have they arrived?*

As spoken Chinese does not reflect gender (though the written Chinese characters are different) it is possible to not know the gender of the person spoken about until they are more completely identified. To denote possession, use the possessive *de* with *tā*:

tā de   *his/her/hers/its*
tā men de   *their/theirs*

Note that the same word can also mean 'him', 'her' or 'them' as an object.

Saying yes

Shì [shr]   *be; is; are*

This word is most commonly used to say 'yes' (i.e. it is so). *Shì* is generally unstressed in a sentence and is used to mark the equivalence between two items (i.e. A *shì* B). As Mandarin does not create tense in the same way as English, *shì* can mean 'am', 'is', 'are', as well as 'was', 'were' or 'will be'. It essentially refers to a state of affairs that exists or has existed or will exist. The expression is also used to indicate agreement. When you mean to disagree it is negated by *bù*:

> *bú shì*   *no; it is not the case*
> *Shì bú shì?*   *Is it the case or not?; Yes or no?* (i.e. use to solicit agreement or an opinion.)
> *Shì ma?*   *Is that so?*
> *Shì tā de ma?*   *Is that his/hers?*
> *Shì wǒ de*   *It is mine.*
> *Shì nǐ de ma?*   *Is it yours?*

Another word commonly used to express agreement is *Duì* [doy] meaning 'that's correct'.

The opposite of *cuò; duì le* is an expression of agreement with what has been said. You may hear the word repeated (by people on the phone), such as: *duì, duì, duì* meaning 'yes, yes, yes, that's right'. See chapter 14 for more on this expression.

Shì can take the (unstressed) possessive particle *de* to become *shì de* meaning 'yes' (certain facts have occurred):

Q: *Tā laí le ma?*   *Has he come?*
A: *Shì de*   *Yes, he has.*

or

A: *Méi yǒu*   *No, he hasn't.*

Cultural note

The sound *shi* is a distinguishing feature of regional pronunciation with people in the south not used to curling back their tongue to pronounce the 'r' sound that makes the word sound more like 'ssi' when pronounced by speakers of mandarin from southern China. *Shì* is one of the most commonly occurring sounds in Mandarin and over 400 characters have this sound in one of the four tones! Foreign speakers of Chinese who can correctly pronounce *shì* are generally lavishly praised by speakers with southern accents for this singular accomplishment. *Zhong* pronounced as 'zong' is a similar pronunciation challenge. Linguists distinguish nine dialect groups for spoken Chinese and brief exposure to the language as it is spoken will reveal the wide variety of regional accents.

Rén [r + brok<u>en</u>]   *person; human being*
Yǒu rén ma?   *Is there anyone/someone there?*
Rén hěn duō   *There are many people (there).*

When *rén* follows the name of a country it creates a nationality, for example:

Zhōng guó rén   *Chinese (lit. China person)*
Měi guó rén   *American*
Yīng guó rén   *English*

Aò dà lì yà rén   *Australian*
Xīn xī lán rén   *New Zealander*

A list of countries can be found at Appendix B.

Cultural note

The spoken language in its reference to China (**Zhōng guó**) and Chinese people (**Zhōng guó rén**) must take into account a modern geo-political reality that in fact comprises not only the People's Republic of China (**zhōng huá rén mín gōng hé guó**) but also the Republic of China (**zhōng huá mín guó**), which is Taiwan (**tái wān**) as well as an extensive diaspora of overseas Chinese (**huá qiáo**) and foreign nationals of Chinese origin (**huá yì**). People of Chinese descent outside of the mainland of China, commonly use the expression **huá rén** and **huá yǔ** to acknowledge their cultural (rather than national) affinity with China as people and with the language respectively. **Huá** used here derives from **huá xià**, an ancient name for China that literally means 'magnificent', 'splendid' and is also the source of the fanciful expression for China as 'the flowery kingdom'. The origin of the name 'China' derives from 'Chin' which was the original spelling of the Qin dynasty (221–207 BC) under which name China was first unified.

Proverb

Zuò jǐng guān tiān
Be a frog in a well; be limited by one's own world view.

zuò	sit
jǐng	well
guān	look
tiān	sky

A classic tale from the other great work of the Daoist canon, the *Zhuang Zi* (often seen as Chuang Tzu) attributed to a historical figure of the same name (c.369–286 BC). It tells of the meeting between a frog who lived in a well and a turtle who lived in the ocean. Very proud of being the master of a kingdom of tadpoles and insects the frog was dismayed to hear the turtle talk of the vastness of the sea. The tale refers to the shortsightedness that comes from ignorance of the limitations of one's own experience. In contrast with Confucius, the Daoist literature characteristically blends whimsical playfulness with philosophical insight and extols the virtues of authentic individualism free from social restraint and communion with a transcendent reality (*dao*) that still resonate strongly with Chinese people today.

6

Can you speak English?
Nǐ huì shuō yīng wén ma?

huì [hway]   *can; know how to; be able/to have learned to* (do something)
   Wǒ bú huì   *I can't* (do it); *it's beyond me.*
   Nǐ huì ma?   *Can you* (do it)?

Note that *huì* is negated only with *bù* (never with *méi*).

Huì is commonly used in discussions around future events, for example:

   tā huì lái   *he can* (will) *come; is likely to*
   Wǒ bú huì lái   *I cannot/will not come; am unlikely to come*

Depending on the context, *bú huì* by itself can mean an event is unlikely to occur, or is highly improbable. For example:

   Tā lái le ma?   *Has he come?*
   Bú huì.   *No way! That's not possible.*
   shuō [shwor]   *say* (something); *speak; talk; utter*

nǐ shuō   you say (something); *you speak*
tā shuō le   he has spoken
Wǒ méi shuō   I didn't speak/say it.
Tā men yǒu méi yǒu shuō?   Did/have they said it?

Note on verbs

Chinese has a strong preference to create words of two sounds and verbs are often formed by a verb and noun element. In this construction the verb to speak becomes *shuō huà* [hwa] (lit. speak words). Other examples are:

chī fàn   eat food (to eat)
chàng gē   sing song (to sing)
zǒu lù   walk road (to walk)
diào yǔ   angle (for) fish (to fish)

Unless the context is very clear monosyllables are rarely used so as to avoid misunderstanding. These two-syllable phrases can be combined with (and sometimes separated by) other words to create different expressions around the same verb/noun constructions, for example:

Tā bù shuō (huà)   *He is not saying anything.*
Tā méi yǒu shuō (hùa)   *He did not speak/say anything.*
Tā yǒu méi yǒu shuō (huà)   *Did he say anything?*
Tā shì shuō shí huà de rén   *He is someone who speaks the truth.*
Tā bù shuō shí huà   *He is not someone who speaks the truth.*
shí   solid (not hollow)

Written, rather than spoken, language

Wén [w + brok<u>en</u>] refers literally to the written language but is used to refer generally to language in its written as well as spoken form. Related terms include:

wén rén   *man of letters; literary person*
wén yì   *literature and art*
wén xué   *literature*
wén míng   *culture(d)*
wén zì   *written word*

The word *wén* added to a country name creates the name of the language, for example:

Fǎ wén   *French*
Dé wén   *German*
Zhōng wén   *Chinese*
Yīng wén   *English*

Yīng is used to transliterate the word for England (see Chapter 3). It has the literal meaning of brave; heroic (*yīng xióng* [shyong] hero).

Wǒ bú huì (shuo) *zhōng wén*   *I cannot speak Chinese.*

A useful variation is:

Wǒ bú dà huì shuō   *I cannot speak much* (Chinese).
   dà [dah]   *big; great; much*

Related expressions

Wǒ bù dǒng [doong]   *I don't understand*
   dǒng   *to understand*
Nǐ dǒng ma?   *Do you understand?*
Wǒ méi tīng dǒng   *I didn't understand* (what you said).
   tīng   *to hear*
Tā de huà wǒ tīng bù dǒng   *I cannot understand what
   he says.*
Kàn bù dǒng   *I cannot understand* (what I see)
   kàn   *to see*
Tā de zì wǒ kàn bù dǒng   *I cannot understand/read his
   writing.*
   zì [its]   *Chinese written script*

Cultural note

Wén is one of the seminal words in Chinese that refers to culture and establishes writing at the centre of the Chinese understanding of civilization. Originally referring to the first man made markings in China (on tortoise shell used for divination) that were the origins of the written language, by extension the word can mean refined and elegant. The word appears in the Chinese term for civilization **wén huà** (lit. literize) and refers to all things literary and cultural that reflects the significance of the written word as a sign of culture and civilization.

In cultural terms the word **wén** is paired with the word **wǔ**: military and by extension warlike, violent, fierce and awesome. Reflecting the Confucian conviction that the pen is mightier than the sword Chinese officialdom was traditionally divided into two ranks, the civil officials who stood on the emperor's left and the military officials who stood on the right—'presiding at court the leader honours the left; resorting to war he honours the right' (*Dao De Jing*, Chapter 31). The divide between civil and military culture is still observable today. The tradition of the warrior is best preserved in Japan where it finds expression in the term *bushido* (that includes the Chinese character for **wǔ**).

The distinction is also preserved in the Chinese breathing and exercise regime known as **qì gōng** in which the two modes of breath control are the 'warrior's breath' (**wǔ xī**) and the 'scholar's breath' (**wén xī**)—the former forceful, strong and audible; the latter natural, silent and gentle.

Proverb

Làn yú chōng shù

Participate just to make up the numbers.

làn	indiscriminate
yú	a flute
chōng	sufficient
shù	number

During the Warring States period (475–226 BC) a ruler enjoyed the music of an orchestra of flute players who were all treated very well on account of their skills. A man called Nan Guo, eager for an easy life, managed to join their ranks by convincing the ruler he too could play. The ruler was succeeded by his son who preferred solo performances and fearing exposure Nan guo, as he couldn't really play, was forced to leave. The saying now refers to anyone with no actual skill but whose presence is required only to make up the numbers. It is also used to refer to incompetent people or inferior goods.

7

Let me invite you to dinner
Wó qíng nǐ chī fàn

qǐng [ching]   request; ask; invite; please

A most useful expression that is the origin of the English expression 'chin-chin' with which it still bears some relationship in sound and meaning. It is often used to mean 'please' as a polite invitation to someone to do something. When Chinese say 'please' in English they are most often translating this word. When used between two people the first person is understood as 'I invite you.../ request you to...'.

It may also be used as a stand-alone expression in many situations where the context is obvious, for example, at a meal it is understood as 'help yourself'; at an entrance, 'after you'. The use of *qǐng* with any request will make it polite. Other common expressions include:

Qǐng jìn (lái)   *Please come in.*
Qǐng zùo [zwor]   *Please take a seat.*
Qǐng wèn   *May I ask* (you a question)?; *Excuse me?*
Qíng nǐ shuō   *Please say it; Please speak up.*

Qǐng tā shuō   *Please ask him to speak/say it.*

Qǐng yòng   *Please help yourself* (lit. please use).

A useful associated expression is ***qǐng kè*** [ker] 'to invite guests'. This is the closest expression in Chinese to 'having a party'. It appears in expressions like:

Wó qǐng kè   *It's my treat/invitation.*

Tā qǐng kè ma?   *Is it his treat?; Is he paying/footing the bill?*

Nǐ shì wǒ men de kè rén   *You are our guest.*

   kè rén   *visitor; guest*

Eating

chī [chr] ***fàn*** [fahn]   *to eat a meal* (lit. eat cooked rice).

One of the most useful expressions in any language, in Chinese it carries all the cultural weight associated with one of the world's great cuisines and refers to what may be considered the national pastime. It is another example of a two syllable expression using a verb and a closely associated noun (see Chapter 6). Note that it is possible to separate out the elements of this verbal compound—***chī*** means 'eat' + ***fàn*** means 'rice' and can be used alone in other contexts. This is the same for all verb–noun compounds.

Related expressions

hǎo chī   (lit. good to eat) *delicious; tasty; I am enjoying this food*

Hǎo chī ma?   *Is it delicious?* Often used by an attentive host.

Hén hǎo chī   *It's really delicious.* Useful to say to a host.
Bù hǎo chī   *It's not tasty; It's not to my taste.*

The Chinese appetite distinguishes five flavours (**wǔ wèi**):

suān [sw + one]   *sour; tart*
tián [tee + <u>en</u>ter]   *sweet* (also used for a smile or temperament)
kǔ [coo]   *bitter* (also used as description of a hard life)
là [lah]   *hot spicy* (also appropriate of people)
xián [she + en]   *salty*

Cultural note

Eating in China remains an important part of social life and an important aspect of entertaining as a means to showcase Chinese culture. China is justifiably proud of its culinary tradition and the dining table is a respected means of entertaining and hospitality. Extended conversation concerning food is accepted and indeed expected of both host and guest. A favourable impression at the dining table by expressions of hearty enjoyment of food is a welcome sign of appreciation of the hospitality of one's host. Reflecting indirectly a respect for the dining table Chairman Mao said: *gé mìng bú shì qǐng kè chī fàn* (lit. revolution is not inviting guests to eat), making the point that the etiquette associated with the dining table has no place in the bloody business of revolution.

Useful qualifiers for the above adjectives are:

hěn   *very*
   hěn tián   *very sweet*
tài [tie]   *too*
   tài là   *too hot/spicy*
zhēn [djen]   *really*
   zhēn kǔ   *really bitter*

The order of phrases can be inverted depending on your desired emphasis:

Tài xián de wǒ bù chī   *It's too salty I won't eat it.*

This can also be a general statement, as in 'I don't eat food that is too salty'. You could say: *wǒ bù chī tài xián de* to emphasize this.

An important phrase to learn is:

Wǒ bù chī wèi jīng   I don't eat MSG.

Another useful expression related to dining is:

Màn màn chī   *Enjoy your meal* (lit. eat slowly).

This is said by a host to a guest, or when eating with others it is used to excuse oneself from the table when one has finished eating first. Note the order—here the adverb precedes the verb.

Proverb

Yǒu péng zì yuán fāng lái bú yì lè hù

What a delight to have friends come from afar.

yǒu	there is/are
péng	friend
zì	from
yuán	far
fāng	place
lái	come
bú yì lè hù	is it not delightful!

A well known expression included in the opening lines of *The Analects of Confucius*. The Master said, 'To learn something and then to put it into practice at the right time: is this not a joy? To have friends coming from afar: is this not a delight? Not to be upset when one's merits are ignored: is this not the mark of a gentleman?' The collection of sayings was compiled by disciples after Confucius' death around 400 BC. Confucian thought originally emphasized moral attainment and ability over birth as conferring the right to rule over others. For use of this quotation see page 102.

8

Who is he?

Tā shì shuí?

Who?

Shuí? [sh + r<u>ay</u>]   *Who?*

The structure is literally he/she is who? Hence you can also say:

Nǐ shì shuí?   *Who are you?*
Shuí lái le?   *Who came?*
Shì shuí de?   *Whose is it?*

What?

Another important question word is:

Shénme? [shemma]   *What?*

Used alone this can mean 'What did you say?' or 'What do you mean?' Or it can be used as an exclamation 'What!'.

The word is composed of two syllables with the latter *me* unstressed.

> *Tā shuō shénme?* *What did he say?; What is he saying?*

It can also be used in response to an expression of thanks:

> *Méi shénme* *That's all right; It's nothing.* (Never use *bù*.)
> For example:

> *A: Xiè xie nǐ* *Thank you very much.*
> *B: Méi shénme* *Not at all.*

> *Shénme yì si?* *What does it mean?; What's it all about?*
> > *yì si* *meaning* (*si* is unstressed)
> > *bù hǎo yì si* *feel embarrassed; ill at ease.* This can also be used to offer a polite apology, as in 'I'm sorry'; 'Let me apologize'; 'Please excuse me (for what I did)'.
> > *Wǔ bù dǒng nǐ de yì si* *I don't know what you mean.*

Why?

When paired with *wèi*, *shénme* is also used to ask 'Why?':

> *Wèi* [way] *shénme?* *Why? Why is it so? How come?*
> > *Nǐ wèi shénme bù shuō?* *Why don't you speak?*
> > *Tā wèi shénme bù dǒng?* *Why doesn't he understand?*
> > *Nǐ men wèi shénme bù chī?* *Why don't/aren't you eat/eating?*

Tā men wèi shénme bù gāo xìng? *Why aren't they happy?*

Tā wèi shénme bù lái? *Why isn't he coming? Why doesn't he come?*

Tā wèi shénme qù le? *Why did he go? Is he going?*

Where?

Shénme dì [dee] *fang* [fung]*?* *Where?* (lit. what place). (*Fang* is unstressed.)

dì fāng *place*

Tā qù shénme dì fang? *Where is he going?* (lit. he goes what place?) is an alternative.

Nǐ qù le shénme dì fang? *Where did you go?*

Note that another word commonly used for 'where' is *nǎli* [nah + lee] or *nǎr* [nahr] in northern accented pronunciation. It can be used interchangeably with *shénme dì fang*, though being shorter it carries slightly less emphasis. For example:

Tā qù nǎr? *Where is he going?*

Nǐ zài nǎr? *Where are you?*

Nǐ shì nǎr de rén? *Where are you from?* (lit. person of where?)

When?

As well as 'what', 'why' and 'where', *shénme* can be used to ask 'when?':

Shénme shí [shr] *hou* [hoh] *When?* (lit. what time). (Note
that *hou* is unstressed.)

Nǐ shénme shí hou qù zhōng guó? *When are you
going to China?*

(Wǒ men) Shénme shí hou dào? *When will (we)
arrive?*

Nǐ shénme shí hou lái? *When do you come?; When
can I expect you?*

Nǐ shì shénme shí hou lái de? *When did you come?*

Wǒ men shénme shí hou chī fàn? *When do we eat?*

Proverb

Zhǐ lù wèi mǎ ────────

Call a stag a horse.

zhǐ	point at
lù	a stag
wèi	consider as
mǎ	horse

This proverb stems from a story from the turbulent time of
the second emperor of the Qin dynasty. In 209 BC he
succeeded his father who had unified China. His prime
minister Zhao Gao had been a high official to his father
and wielded real authority in the court. To test the loyalty
of the new emperor's ministers Zhao Gao presented a stag
to the emperor insisting that it was a fine horse and
challenged the officials to dispute his assertion so as to
identify his opponents. He was eventually responsible for
the assassination of the new emperor.

The proverb is used to refer to any deliberate distortion
or misrepresentations of the truth, or can also refer to agreeing
with whatever your boss says, no matter how ridiculous.

9

What time is it now?

Xiàn zài jí diǎn?

xiàn [sea + <u>end</u>] *zài* [dz + eye]   *now; at the present time*
  Xiàn zài hǎo ma?   *Is now OK/fine?* (Is it all right to do something now? Let's do it now OK?)
  Xiàn zài hǎo le ma?   *Is it better?* (Has the situation improved?)
  Nǐ xiàn zài qù ma?   *Are you going now?*
  Nǐ xiàn zài qù shénme dì fang?   *Where are you going now?*
Jí [gee] *diǎn* [dee + <u>end</u>]   *What time is it?* (lit. how many dots?)

Time is one of the most practical uses for counting in Chinese and provides a useful introduction to numbers. Take a look at the table below:

Number		Time		Counting objects*	
yī†	one	*yì diǎn*	1 o'clock	*yí gè*	one (object)
èr	two	*liáng diǎn‡*	2 o'clock	*liǎng gè‡*	two...
sān	three	*sān diǎn*	3 o'clock	*sān gè*	three...

Number		**Time**		**Counting objects***	
sì	four	*sì diăn*	4 o'clock	*sì gè*	four…
wŭ	five	*wú diăn*	5 o'clock	*wŭ gè*	five…
liù	six	*liù diăn*	6 o'clock	*liù gè*	six…
qī	seven	*qī diăn*	7 o'clock	*qī gè*	seven…
bā	eight	*bā diăn*	8 o'clock	*bā gè*	eight…
jiŭ	nine	*jiú diăn*	9 o'clock	*jiŭ gè*	nine…
shí	ten	*shí diăn*	10 o'clock	*shí gè*	ten…
shí yī	eleven	*shí yì diăn*	11 o'clock	*shí yí gè*	eleven…
shí èr	twelve	*shí èr diăn*	12 o'clock	*shí èr gè*	twelve…

* Counting objects requires another particle (generally called a classifier) that specifies the type of object spoken about. *Gè* [g + <u>her</u>] is the most commonly used classifier. The sound is unstressed. For example, if you were speaking about the number of people you would say: *yí ge rén* one person, a person; *liăng ge rén* two people, etc.

† While *yi* is a first tone its actual pronunciation as noted in the text depends on the tone of the following word—rising second tone before a falling fourth tone; a fourth tone before a second or a third.

‡ 'Two' is the only number that changes depending on context. The word for 'two' is *èr* while for counting and time you use *liăng* [lee + ung].

Cultural note

As in many other cultures, the power of numbers exerts a particular fascination in China where numerical harmony is understood to obey fixed but ultimately mysterious laws. Certain numbers, for example *liù* (6), has sound associations with being smoothly flowing and hence is connected to prosperity and success. Similarly *bā* (8) sounds like *fa* that appears as *fā cái* which means to get rich and which is represented in the common new year greating *gōng xǐ fā cái* (or seen as *kong hee fat choi* in accordance with Cantonese pronunciation). The number *sì* (4) is to be avoided because it has the same sound as the word for death.

Lucky or auspicious numbers are eagerly sought to be incorporated into transactions of all kinds whether it be the height of buildings, telephone numbers or vehicle number plates. It comes as little surprise that the Beijing Olympic clock has been ticking down to 08.08.2008.

Series of numbers read together can be given particularly auspicious readings and in the age of email and SMS such associations have taken on new dimensions.

Personal names and numbers come together in the number of strokes used to write the character used in the name which should be a 'good number'.

More on counting

Counting is logical and reflects the economy of the Chinese language sound structure. It is a useful way to practice distinguishing tones.

There is a logic to expressing larger numbers in Mandarin:

shí sì   *fourteen* (ten four)

shí qī   *seventeen* (ten seven)

   èr shí   (two ten) *twenty* [never *liǎng shí*] Twenty is special in this regard.

   wǔ shí liù   *fifty six* (five ten six)

   qī shí qī   *seventy seven*

Counting larger numbers follows the same basic logic:

> *bǎi* [buy]   *hundred*
> > *Yì bǎi*   *100*
> > *liáng bǎi*   *200*
> > *sān bǎi*   *300*
> > *sì bǎi*   *400...*
>
> *qiān* [chee + <u>end</u>]   *thousand*
> > *Yì qiān*   *1000*
> > *liǎng qiān*   *2000*
> > *sān qiān*   *3000...*
>
> *wàn* [wun]   *ten thousand*
> > *Yí wàn*   *10 000*
> > *liǎng wàn*   *20 000*
> > *sān wàn*   *30 000...*
>
> *Yì bǎi wàn*   *1 million* (i.e. 1 000 000)
> > *liáng bǎi wàn*   *2 million*
> > *sān bǎi wàn*   *3 million...*
> > *Yì qiān wàn*   *10 million*
> > *liǎng qiàn wan*   *20 million...*
>
> *Yí yì*   *100 million* (i.e. 100 000 000)

More on time

> *fēn* [orphan] is the word used for minute.
> > *Sān diǎn èr shí fēn*   *3.20*
> > *Sì diǎn sì shí wǔ fēn*   *4.45*

zhōng (lit. clock) is also a word that can be used to follow *diǎn*:

Wǒ sì diǎn zhōng lái *I will come at four o'clock.*

Tā shuō tā qī diǎn zhōng dào *He said/says he will arrive at 7.*

Cultural Note

As the word for clock (**zhōng**) has the same sound as a word meaning 'to end' and hence 'to die' clocks are never presented as gifts. 'To give a clock' (**sōng zhōng**) has the same sound as words that mean 'to escort the body to the grave'!

While China had an indigenous clock-making tradition extending over the 10th to 14th centuries the Chinese were fascinated by the first European clocks (their small size being a particular attraction) that were introduced by Jesuit missionaries in 1583. A horological workshop was later established at the Chinese court and was staffed by missionaries for nearly two centuries.

Bàn [bun] is the word for half:

Tā sān diǎn bàn qù *He will go at 3.30.*

Note the word order: subject + time words + verb. This is in keeping with the general sense of order that Chinese grammar imposes on sentence structure that also allows for great flexibility while giving prime place to what is considered most important. In the above example you could also say: ***sān diǎn bàn tā qù*** if an emphasis on the time was required.

Other time words:

jīn tiān [tee + <u>end</u>]   *today*

  tiān   *sky; heaven*

míng tiān   tomorrow
zuó [zwor] *tiān*   yesterday
zǎo [dz + cow] shàng [sh + hung]   morning
xià [she + uh] wǔ [woo]   afternoon
wǎn [wahn] shàng   evening; night
Tā jīn tiān (wǎn shàng) qù   He is going today (this
  evening).
Wǒ míng tiān (shàng wǔ) lái   I will come tomorrow
  (afternoon).

The role of time words to create tense should also
be noted:

Wǒ jīn tiān lái   I am coming today.
Tā míng tiān qù ma?   Will he go tomorrow?
Nǐ zuó tiān lái le ma?   Did you come yesterday?

Time of year

jì jié   the seasons
chūn [chwoon] *tiān*   spring
xià [she + ya] *tiān*   summer
qiū [chee + you] *tiān*   autumn
dōng [o as in cook] *tiān*   winter
  Xiàn zài shi chūn tiān   It's spring now.
  Běi jīng de dōng tiān hén lěng   Winter in Beijing is cold.
  Qiū tiān hěn shū fu   Autumn is pleasant (lit. comfortable).
  Wǒ men de guó jiā xià tiān bú rè   Summer is not hot in
    our country.
  Jì jié bú ràng rén   The seasons do not wait for (farming)
    people (i.e. Time waits for no man).

The four seasons are colloquially referred to in the order: *chūn xià qiū dōng.*

While perhaps not as much as in the past China still identifies itself as an agricultural country with each season distinguished by particular activities. Seasonal change is reflected in food as well as clothing. Polite conversation about the seasons is frequent and often extended. Needless to say, using the qualities of the seasons as metaphors is equally extensive. Such usage is reflected in the following common sayings:

> *Huā dào chūn tiān zì rán kāi*   Flowers in spring naturally
> blossom (i.e. things develop naturally in their own time).
> *Yì nián zhī jì zài yú chūn*   One year's plan [depends on]
> spring (i.e. success depends on a good beginning).

Days of the week and months of the year are created by the use of the ordinal number sets preceded by the words for 'week' either *lǐ bài* or *xīng qī,* or the word for 'month' *yuè* [you + end] as follows:

Lǐ bài yī	Monday	*yí ge lǐ bài*	one week
Lǐ bài èr	Tuesday	*liǎng ge lǐ bài*	two weeks
Lǐ bài sān	Wednesday	*sān ge lǐ bài*	three weeks
Lǐ bài sì	Thursday	*sì ge lǐ bài*	four weeks
Lǐ bài wǔ	Friday	*wǔ ge lǐ bài*	five weeks
Lǐ bài liù	Saturday	*liù ge lǐ bài*	six weeks
*Lǐ bài tiān	Sunday	*qī ge lǐ bài*	seven weeks

*Sunday is the exception in not being followed by a number

Months of the year follow the same principle:

Yí yuè	*January*	**yí ge yuè**	*one month*
Èr yuè	*February*	**liǎng ge yuè**	*two months*
Sān yuè	*March*	**Sān ge yuè**	*three months*
Sì yuè	*April*	**sì ge yuè**	*four months*
Wǔ yuè	*May*	**wǔ ge yuè**	*five months*

The word for year *nián* [knee + <u>any</u>] follows the same principle:

jīn nián	*this year*	**yì nián**	*one year*
			(never *yi ge nian*)
míng nián	*next year*	**liǎng nián**	*two years*
qù nián	*last year*	**sān nián**	*three years*

Proverb

Wǔ shí bù xiào bǎi bù

(Those who retreat) fifty paces laugh at (those who retreat) one hundred paces. (i.e. the pot calling the kettle black)

wǔ shí	fifty
bù	pace
xiào	laugh/at
bǎi bù	a hundred paces

This is a well-known quotation from Mencius (372–289 BC), who is considered second only to Confucius as a moralist and philosopher. The record of his teachings, in the form of conversations with rulers who sought his advice, are also included among the Confucian *Four Books* (**sì shū**) that were among the first texts memorized by students in imperial China.

This expression refers to soldiers defeated in a battle who retreat fifty paces and ridicule those who retreat a hundred paces. It is presented by Mencius as an analogy in the course of advice on the principles of good government to a ruler who is concerned he derives no obvious benefit from his policies that he compares with those of his neighbours. Mencius makes the point that comparisons are worthless in cases where each party has the same faults—differing only in degrees.

10

I like to eat Chinese food
Wó xǐ huan chī zhōng cān

xǐ [she] ***huan*** [hwan]   *like; like to; love; be fond of; keen on; enjoy.* (Note that ***huan*** is unstressed.)

This is an extremely useful way to express likes in a general sense. For example:

> *Wó xǐ huan tā*   *I like him/her.*
> **Q:** *Nǐ bù xǐ huan ma?*   *You don't like* (it)?
> **A:** *Bù, wó xǐ huan*   *No, I like it.*
> *Tā xǐ huan chī shénme?*   *What does he/she like to eat?*

zhōng [djoong] ***cān*** [<u>its</u> + <u>un</u>der]   *Chinese food*

Zhōng is used here as an abbreviation for China (i.e. ***Zhōng guó***); ***cān*** is another word for food or, more specifically, a meal.

Related expressions show the flexibility of word creation in Chinese by the linking of related components:

> *wǔ* [woo] ***cān***   *lunch*
> ***cān chē*** [ch + <u>early</u>]   *dining car* (on a train)

cān tīng   *dining room; restaurant*
cān jīn   *table napkin*
Xī cān   *Western food*

A closely related expression that is often used is **cài** [ts + eye] which also refers to a dish or course of food. Chinese food is customarily shared with all courses served together. Each course is referred to as **cài**. Its original meaning is 'vegetable' and it is used in expressions like:

zhōng guó cài   *Chinese food*
qīng cài   *green vegetable*
cài dān   *menu*
Chuān [chew + <u>und</u>er] **cài**   *Sichuan style food*
Wó xǐ huan (chi) **zhè ge cài**   *I like this dish.*

A useful qualifying expression is **tè bié** [bee + air] *especially; particularly.*

Tā tè bié xǐ huan chī zhōng cān   *He is especially fond of Chinese food.*

Adding the possessive particle *de* makes the following possible:

Wó xǐ huan chī là de (cài)   *I like spicy (food).*
Tā xǐ huan chī tián de   *He/she likes sweet (food).*
Q: *Nǐ bù xǐ huan chī xī cān ma?*   *You don't like Western food?*
A: *Shì, wǒ bú dà xǐ huan*   *That's right, I don't like it much.*

A related expression at the dining table often used by the attentive host is:

(*Qíng nǐ*) *Duō* (duō) *chī* (cài)   (*Please*) *eat more.*
   duō [door]   *much; many; more*

Equally important on many dining occasions are the expressions:

Wó (*chī*) *bǎo* [bough] *le*   *I am full; I have had enough to eat.*
Nǐ chī bǎo le ma?   *Have you had enough? Are you full?*
Tā méi chī bǎo   *He is not full; He hasn't eaten enough.*

Cultural note

It is not unexpected or unwelcome for a guest or visitor to make gratuitous remarks of a complimentary nature and one of the best times to do this is when dining with locals. Compliments and flattering remarks are an important and useful aspect of social intercourse worldwide, not least of all among Chinese who are past masters at the well turned compliment—and it goes without saying—the well timed barb. A saying has it that flattery brings fortune while honest speech buys trouble (*Ē yú yǒu fú, zhí yán gǔ huò*).

An important aspect of the art of polite conversation is saying what is *hǎo tīng*—good to hear—from the listener's point of view, especially when you have bad or unwelcome news. Needless to say, euphemism and circumlocution also find their way into the translation of much polite exchange—not always felicitously. Complimentary language is a useful addition to the most elementary vocabulary as it helps to meaningfully enhance social relations. As a visitor it is always appropriate to make complimentary remarks on China, its people—and, perhaps most of all, the food!

Proverb

Jí suǒ bú yù, wù shī yú rén
What you do not wish for yourself,
do not do to others.

jǐ	self
suǒ	which
bù	not
yù	desire
wù	do not
shī	do
yú	towards
rén	people

China's classic expression of the Golden Rule (expressed in the negative) as it appears in *The Analects of Confucius* as follows:

One of Confucius' disciples asked,

'Is there a single word that could guide one's entire life?'

The Master replied, 'Should it not be *reciprocity*? What you do not wish for yourself, do not do to others.' (15.24; Leys trans.)

This is another of the sayings of Confucius that continue to be well known today even if its source is not.

The Chinese word used for recipriocity is **shù** that literally means 'to show consideration for others'. It is still used in highly polite language to mean 'excuse me, I must leave now' as in the expression **shù bú fèng péi** which means 'please excuse me for not keeping you company'.

11

May I? OK?

Ké yǐ ma?

ké [ker] *yǐ* [ee]   *may; can*

This expression has a wide variety of usages including to indicate a request or permission and hence that something is 'all right', 'OK', 'may/can'.

Wǒ ké yǐ qù ma?   *May I go? Is it OK if I go?*
Ké yǐ   *It's OK; All right.*

It also has a broader meaning and can be used as an enthusiastic expression of approval:

Nǐ zhēn ké yǐ   *You are really great/terrific.*
Nǐ de yīng wén hěn ké yǐ   *Your English is pretty good.*

A closely related colloquial expression to indicate that something is OK or all right (to do) is *xíng [shing]* (lit. to go). For example:

Xíng ma?   *Is it OK (to do this)? Will this work/do?*
Bù xíng   *It's not OK; That won't do; That's not possible.*

By extension a useful complementary expression is:

Nǐ zhēn xíng *You're really terrific* (competent)

Another word that can often be interchanged with *ké yǐ* in the sense of 'being able'; is *néng* [n + he̲r + ng] which has the meaning of ability, capability or skill. Thus it is possible to make the following requests:

Wǒ néng qù ma? *Can/may I go?*
Nǐ néng zuò ma? *Are you able to do it?*
Tā míng tiān bù néng lái *He cannot come tomorrow.*

Please note that where someone has an ability as a result of having learned something then *huì* is used (see Chapter 6).

Another frequently used expression with *kě* that is used to express strong agreement with what has just been said is:

Kě bú shì ma *You can say that again!; Of course!* (lit. can it be that it is not so?)

Related expressions

Néng géi wǒ yī diǎn (shuǐ) ma? *May I have some (water)?*
gěi [gay] *give, grant*
Wó yǒu yì dián kě *I am a little thirsty.*
   Yì diǎn [dee + e̲nd] *A little bit.* This is a very useful qualifying expression (*yì diǎr* in northern pronunciation).
Qǐng géi wǒ yì diǎn *Give me a little please.*

Wŏ huì shuō yī diăn zhōng wén   *I speak a little Chinese.*
kĕ [ker]   *to be thirsty*
　Ní kĕ le ma?   *Are you thirsty?*

Used in front of the negative *bù* the expression *yì diăn* can be used to mean 'not at all' (i.e. to express strong disagreement). For example:

(Wŏ) yì diăn bù kĕ   *I am not thirsty at all.*
Tā yì diăn bú lèi   *She's not tired at all.*
　lèi [lay]   *tired*
Yì diăn bù xĭ huan   *(I) don't like it at all.*
Yì diăn bù gāo xing   *(He's) not happy at all.*
Yì diăn bù xíng   *That won't work at all.*

Requests

Associated expressions for polite requests include:

xiăng   *want to; would like to; feel like, to miss*
　Ní xiăng qù ma?   *Do you feel like going?*
　Tā bù xiăng lái   *He doesn't want to come.*
　Wŏ hén xiăng tā   *I miss him/her.*
　　Wó xiăng [see + ung] hē [her] kā fēi [kah fay]   *I would like to drink a coffee;* or simply *kā fēi (nĭ) yŏu ma?*   *Do you have/Is there any coffee?*

Other beverages commonly encountered:

chá	*tea*	*shuĭ*	*water*
jiŭ	*wine*	*kĕ lè*	*cola*
pí jiŭ	*beer*	*qì shuĭ*	*soft drink* (lit. aerated water)

A more direct (and hence less polite) request can be made using:

Wǒ yào [y̱et + cow] *I want* (it)

Yào is another basic expression with a wide variety of usages whose original meaning is 'important' or 'essential' and by implication refers to a want, wish or desire. It can be used to ask someone for something, while it also has an imperative meaning as 'must' or 'should', as well as 'shall', 'will' or 'be going to'. It is also one of those words in the language that has a great etymological load bearing capacity and the dictionary entries for its usage are extensive and varied, ranging from *yào rén* (important person) to *yào fàn* (to beg food), while *yào miàn zi* means to want to keep up appearances (lit. to want face).

Most usefully this expression can be used to refuse requests and express dislike:

Xiè xie (wǒ) bú yào *No thanks!* (i.e. I don't want/to do it)
Wǒ bú yào qù *I don't want to go*
Tā bú yào chī ma? *Doesn't he want to eat it?*
Nǐ men bú yào shuō ma? *Don't you want to speak?*
Wǔ bú yào hē kā fēi, wó xiǎng hē chá *I don't want coffee, I'd like some tea.*
Ní xiǎng yào shénme? *What would you like?*
Tā xiǎng hē shénme? *What would he like to drink?*

Important related expressions:

hē zuì [dzway] *get drunk*
Wǒ hē zuì le *I'm drunk.*

Nǐ bú yào hē zuì. *Don't get drunk.*

Wǒ bú yào hē zuì. *I don't want to get drunk.*

A useful expression to regulate the toasting importunities of your drinking companions is:

Suí [sway] ***yì*** *as you like; at will; as one pleases*

This is a polite signal to drink as little as you feel like. Usually repeated as *suí yì suí yì*.

Cultural note

Drinking wine and highly alcoholic Chinese spirits can be an important part of socializing in China, not least of all as part of official hospitality.

Like food, much etiquette has evolved around drinking and toasting. At a dinner, drinking is never done as an individual pleasure but an opportunity to share in the form of proposing toasts to one or many of the guests at the table. Official dining provides ample opportunity to both the host and the guests to express any manner of sentiments in the context of one's role as host or guest.

A wordless inclination of one's glass in anyone's direction is usually sufficient indication of intent and readily understood.

Various attitudes to drinking find expression in a host of sayings such as the following:

Jiǔ féng zhī jǐ qiān zhōng shǎo   When drinking with friends, a thousand cups are too few.

Jīn zhāo yóu jiǔ jīn zhāo zuì   literally today we have wine so let's get drunk (a classic expression from a Tang poem of *carpe diem*, enjoy the present)

Jiŭ néng chéng shì jiŭ néng bài shì   (Drinking) wine can accomplish things [and] wine can ruin things (things can be either settled or ruined by wine).

The simplest verbal expression to use to propose a toast is *gān* [gahn] *bēi* [bay] It means 'bottoms up' literally 'dry glass', but don't feel compelled to do this! The usual formula for toasting is:

> *Wèi...(gān bēi)*   *I propose a toast to...*

It should be noted that the *gān bēi* can be omitted.

wèi [way]   *for; for the benefit of*
> *Wèi wŏ men de yŏu yì (gan bei)*   *To our friendship.*
> *Wèi dà jiā de jiàn kāng*   *To everyone's health.*
> *Wèi wŏ men de chéng gōng*   *To our success.*
> *Wèi yóu hăo hé zuò guān xi de fā zhăn*   *To the development of* (our) *friendly cooperative relations.*

Zhù [george + oo] *nĭ jiàn* [gee + end] *kāng* [k + hung]   *To your good health.*
> *zhù*   here used to mean *wishing/hoping*

Proverb

Bù shí lù shān zhēn miàn mù

*No one knows the true face of Mt. Lu
(i.e. not being able to see things
objectively).*

bù	not
shí	know
lù shān	Mt. Lu
zhēn	true
miàn	face
mù	eye

A line from a poem by the famous Song dynasty poet and scholar Sù Shī (1037–1101 AD) used to indicate that one is too close to the subject to be objective and so does not really know what one is talking about.

> Ridges are seen in front and peaks at the side
> Far or near, high or low each is different.
> No one knows the true face of Mt Lu,
> Who find themselves within the mountain.

While not one of China's five sacred mountains, Mt. Lu in Jiang xi Province has always been a favourite subject with landscape painters as well as poets and is still a popular scenic attraction today.

12

We are old friends

Wŏ men shì lăo péng you

shì [shr]   *be; is; are* (see Chapter 5)
  lăo [l + c<u>ow</u>]   *be old; elderly*

Wŏ men shì lăo péng you has a variety of cultural usages. It is often used to precede a surname as a sign of respect and as an indication of friendship, particularly among colleagues and classmates, for example *Lăo Wáng*. It also reflects the preference for avoiding the use of personal names which are considered too intimate (and hence personal names are used mainly within the family). In this sense of old it means the opposite of 'new'—*xīn* [shin]

Cultural note

Next to expressions of hospitality, remarks concerning friendship and general cordial relations can never be too effusive. Such sentiments are variously expressed in even the most informal and formal settings.

Relations between individuals (notably perceptions of relative status), institutions and indeed nations can be defined and expressed in similar terms. 'You are an old friend of China…' is a well-meant (if hackneyed) compliment, whether or not it is grounded in substance. The expression of the compliment may be a desire to see some evidence of its reality.

Related expressions

> **Láo bǎn** [bahn]   *boss;* owner of a business; also a term of address

As an expression common before 1949 and the founding of the PRC *láo bǎn* has had pejorative connotations. Today it has become acceptable and is sometimes used (half) jokingly to refer to the person in authority. It can be used as a sign of respect to someone (usually male) to exaggerate some minor or actual authority.

> **Nǐ shì láo bǎn**   *You're the boss!*
> **Wáng láo bǎn lái le**   *Wang the boss is coming.*
> **Tā shì wǒ men de láo bǎn**   *He's our boss.*
> **dà láo bǎn**   *big boss*
> **xiǎo láo bǎn**   *'little' boss* (boss of a single person business)
> **lǎo rén**   *elderly person*
> **lǎo shī**   *teacher* (as a form of direct address); can be used as a term of respect (e.g. **Wáng lǎo shī**)
> **lǎo wài** [why]   the most common expression now used to refer to a foreigner (lit. old outside)
>> **wài guo rén**   the formal expression for foreigner (lit. outside country person)

The complimentary expression to someone younger is *xiǎo* [see + ow] (lit. small; little).

Xiǎo Wáng   *a friendly term of address to Mr/Ms Wang*

Xiǎo péng you   (lit. small friend) *a common form of direct address to children*

Xiǎo features in other expressions as well:

Xiǎo xīn   *Be careful; watch out!*

Nǐ yào xiǎo xīn   *You should be careful.*

Xiáo jiě [gee + eh]   *Miss; young lady. Jiě* (lit. elder sister) is unstressed.

The above term can be used to address staff, for example, to attract the attention of a waitress or to speak of young woman in the the third person as an alternative to *tā*. Usage of the expression today should tempered by the fact that informally it is now also used as slang for a female prostitute.

Xiǎo fèi [fay]   *tip* (given to a waiter etc.)

Xiǎo qì [chee]   *be stingy; petty*

   Tā hén xiǎo qì   *He's stingy*

Xiǎo biàn [bee + end]   *urinate* (lit. small convenience)

   Wǒ yào xiǎo biàn   *I want to take a pee.*

Friendship

Péng [p + sing] **you** [yet + oh]   *friend* (*you* is unstressed)

   Wǒ men shì hǎo péng you   *We are good friends.*

   Nǐ shì wǒ de péng you   *You are my friend.*

Nǐ shì tā men de péng you ma?   *Are you a friend of theirs?*
Xiǎo péng you shì shuí?   *Who are you, little friend?*
    (addressed to a child)
nǚ péng you   *girlfriend*
nán péng you   *boyfriend*
    Tā yǒu nán péng you ma?   *Does she have a boyfriend?*
jiǔ ròu péng you   *fair weather friends* (lit. 'wine meat friends'—those who are around only when there is free food).

Related expressions

yǒu yì   *friendship*
Yǒu yì dì yī   *Friendship comes first.*

A useful phrase for a toast is:

Wèi wǒ men de yǒu yì gān bēi   *Let's drink to our friendship.*

Cultural note

Associations of friendship with China's foreign relations have had a varied provenance since 1949.

The expression of the precedence of friendship in foreign relationships is associated with the slogan *yǒu yì dì yī bǐ sài* [sigh] *dì èr* (friendship first competition second) which is a reminder of the less competitive days when China's sporting and diplomatic activities coincided and pre-dated China's arrival on the international sporting scene. The first part of this slogan (friendship first) has proved to be more enduring.

While *Yǒu yì shāng diàn*   *Friendship Store* is now just the name of another department store in China's large cities, these were originally the dedicated consumer precinct for foreign visitors (friends) to China and the envy of local residents. While the name continues to exist as a reminder of China's socialist past, their prominence ended in the early 1980s and state ownership has been corporatized.

yóu hǎo   *friendly; amicable*
Tā hěn yóu hǎo   *He is very friendly.*
Tài bù yóu hǎo!   *most unfriendly*
bú tài yóu hǎo   *not too friendly*

Proverb

Cǐ dì wú yín sān bái liǎng

Three hundred taels of silver is not buried here (i.e. a dead give away).

cǐ	this
dì	place
wú	without
yín	silver
sān	three
bái	hundred
liǎng	chinese weight measure

This proverb refers to a popular fable of a man who thought he was very clever. When he came into possession of a large sum of money he buried the money in his yard and put up a sign above the spot. The story continues that the man's neighbour, who was a thief, also put up a sign in his yard reading 'I have not stolen anything'. The saying refers to action taken to cover something up that only makes it more obvious as in a very poor lie (or denial) which only reveals the truth of a matter or of a guilty person who gives himself away by conspicuously protesting his innocence. It is a good example of the kind of irony that characterizes Chinese humour.

13

Beijing is beautiful
Běijīng hěn piào liang

Piào [pee + c<u>ow</u>] **liang** [lee + h<u>ung</u>]   *be handsome; pretty; attractive; good looking* (**liang** is unstressed here).

This adjective can be used for people as well as certain material objects.

It is a useful exclamation of admiration in the sense of remarkable, brilliant and splendid (e.g. a brilliant victory, beautiful Chinese, a beautiful home run). Adjectives can be made nouns by the simple addition of *de* (unstressed) for example:

Wǒ xǐ huan piào liang de   *I like* (the) *pretty one(s)*

A related expression is **měi** [may] **lì** [lee]   *beautiful; fine; artistic*

Hén měi   *It's beautiful!*

It can be used to remark on beautiful scenery. And it is used in the word for fine art, **měi shù** [shoo], and **měi shù guǎn** [gwahn] means 'art gallery'.

Chinese has a preference to frequently qualify adjectives with the addition of *bǐ jiào*, 'to compare'. This gives the sense of 'pretty, fairly, rather' such as:

> *bǐ jiào hǎo*   *pretty good*
> *bǐ jiào piào liang*   *rather beautiful*

Useful complimentary remarks that in fact are often used by Chinese to describe what they themselves see as their own characterisitic virtues include:

> *Zhōng guó rén hěn hào kè*   *Chinese are very hospitable.*
> *qín* [chin] *láo*   *hardworking*
> *cōng* [its + look + ng] *míng*   *intelligent*
> *néng gàn* [gun]   *capable*
> *pú sù*   *plain/simple in one's tastes*
> *hán xù*   *restrained; modest; reserved*
> *yōu mò* [more]   *funny; humorous*
> *shàn liáng*   *kind; good*
> *hào kè* [ker]   *hospitable* (lit. to enjoy guests)
> *kè*   *guest; visitor*
> *Tā shì kè rén*   *He is a visitor/a guest.*
> *kè qi*   *be polite* (lit. guest air), *qi* is unstressed
>> *Tā hěn kè qi*   *He is polite.*
>> *Nǐ tài kè qi*   *You are too polite.*
>> *Nǐ bié kè qi*   *Please don't stand on ceremony; Please make yourself at home* (to host); *Please don't bother/fuss.*
>> *bié* [bee + air]   *do not*

Bú kè qi (lit. not polite) may be used as a stand alone response to an expression of thanks to mean: *You're welcome; Don't mention it; Please don't bother.*

Note that the expression can also be used in its original meaning:

Tā hěn bú kè qi *He is/was not very polite; he's rude.*

Cultural note

The distinction between guest (*kè rén*) and host (*zhǔ rén*) has a long tradition in China, reinforced by both culture and a history which provides many examples of the expected behaviour as well as that considered to be in breach of etiquette.

Correct behaviour is enshrined as one of the Confucian virtues known as *lǐ*, which after humanity and justice is the most important of the Five Constant Virtues (*wǔ cháng*), along with intelligence and trust, that define ethical relations. In Confucian practice every interaction between people exhibits these defining characteristics.

Courtesy demands the guest show deference to the host who is expected to display a polite concern for the well being of the guest to whom he has a responsibility. A guest is well advised to bear in mind the saying that 'a strong guest does not pressure his host' (*qiáng bīn bù yā zhǔ*) by neither displaying superiority nor challenging any possibly contentious views. Host and guest relationships are tempered by the knowledge of a future time when roles may well be reversed. The classic formulation of protocol is *lǐ shàng wǎng lái*—propriety involves give and take; courtesy demands reciprocity.

More compliments

Nǐ de gōng xiàn hěn dà   You've made a great contribution.
Wó hěn pèi fu nǐ/zhōng guó rén   I admire you/Chinese.
pèi [pay] *fu* [foo]   admire and respect (*fu* is unstressed).
Wó hěn pèi fu nǐ de chéng gōng   I admire your success.
Nǐ de yóng gǎn   I admire your courage.
Nǐ de nài xīn   I admire your patience.

Nǐ zhēn lì hai!   You're awesome; tremendous; formidable.
(*hai* is unstressed).

The expression *lì hai* has wide application and can also refer to people who are wily, shrewd and subtle. It can be used to describe extreme natural phenomenon (e.g. weather, devastation). When used appropriately this shows a subtle use of the language that may elicit the same comment as one of admiration.

(Nǐ) hén liǎo bù qǐ   (You're) amazing; extraordinary; terrific.

A more literary expression for someone who is outstanding is *Chū lèi bā cuì*, 'In a league of one's own'. It can be used in the following way:

Wáng xiān sheng shi ge chū lèi bā cuì de rén   Mr Wang is an exceptional person.

Proverb

Rén zhī chū xìng běn shàn

Man is born good.

rén	person
zhī	possessive particle
chū	beginning
xìng	nature
běn	original
shàn	good

This saying is the opening line of the *Three Character Classic* (*Sān Zì Jīng*), an elementary guide for Chinese children arranged in 356 alternately rhyming lines of three characters each and containing about 500 characters in total. It became the foundation-stone of Chinese education from its composition in the 13th century as every Chinese child began their study by committing its lines to memory. Many lines remain well known today and modern editions are widely available in most Chinese bookshops.

The opening lines encapsulate the traditional idealistic Confucian view of man and his place in the world. The lines continue, ***xìng xiāng jìn, xí xiāng yuán***—human nature makes men close, with custom they become widely different—expressing the Confucian insight into the nature/culture dichotomy. This view is complemented by that of a rationalist school of thought for which man's nature was considered evil and goodness only acquired by education.

14

No problem!

Méi wèn tí!

Méi is the abbreviation of *méi yŏu*, 'there is no.' (see Chapter 4). While most often used with a verb it may appear alone to mean 'no (there isn't)' in answer to a question, for example 'there is/was no such state of affairs.'

> *Méi yŏu le*   *There is none; it's all gone, all used up; it's out of stock.*

> *wèn*   *to ask; inquire about*
> *wèn tí* [tee]   *problem; issue; question*
> *Wèn tí bù duō*   *There are not many problems* (with this).
> *Wèn tí hĕn duō*   *There are many problems.*
> *Ní yŏu wèn tí ma?*   *Do you have a problem/question?*
> *Tā yŏu wèn tí ma?*   *Does he have a problem?*
> *Wó ké yĭ wèn yí gè wèn tí ma?*   *May I ask a question?*

Related expressions

Nǐ cuò [tswor] **le**   *You are* (in the) *wrong.*

Cuò le   *That's incorrect; not right.*

Wǒ shuō cuò le   *I said the wrong thing; said it incorrectly.*

Méi cuò   *It's/you're right; not wrong.*

bú cuò   *be pretty good; not bad* (of people and things).

Note also:

Duì le ma?   *Is it right? Correct?*

Nǐ shuō duì le   *What you said is correct/right.*

Bú duì (never **méi duì**): *incorrect; wrong; that's not right.*
   This can be used to express disagreement.

Duì has the literal meaning of being face to face with someone and this gives us the expression:

Duì bù qǐ   (lit. I cannot face you) *I am sorry; Excuse me; I beg your pardon.*

The below expression can be used when apologizing to someone as well as when interrupting someone:

Duì bù qǐ, wǒ ké yǐ wèn yī gè wèn tí ma?   *Excuse me may I ask a question?*

Proverb

Zhǐ shàng tán bīng

Be an armchair strategist;
engage in idle theorizing.

zhǐ	paper
shàng	on
tán	talk
bīng	warfare

Recorded in China's earliest comprehensive history the *Records of the Historian* (**Shǐ Jì**) by Sima Qian (c.145–90 BC) in relation to the son of a famous general who was unable to carry out his extravagant claims to military strategy. He died on the battlefield in the 3rd Century BC during China's Warring States period prior to unification under the state of Qin. Sima Qian succeeded his father to the position of Grand Historian and his official history set a standard that was followed throughout imperial times (that ended with the overthrow of the Qing Dynasty in 1911).

15

How do you know that?

Ní zěnme zhī dào?

Zěnme [dz + Emma]   *How? How come? In what way?* The second syllable *me* is unstressed and shorter.

Zěnme shuō?   *How do you say it?*

   (Yòng) zhōng wén zěnme shuō?   *How do you say it in Chinese?*

   ***yòng** [yoong]*   *to use; utilize*

Zěnme qù?   *How do you/shall we go there?*

Zěnme bàn?   *What's to be done; What can we do about this?*

Tā zěnme méi lái?   *How come he didn't come?*

Zěnme le?   *What's wrong? What's happened?*

An extremely useful related (and widely used) colloquial expression is:

Zěnme yàng?   *How are you going? How are things going?*

   ***yàng** [young]*   *appearance; shape*

It can be used to solicit an opinion about some state of affairs, as in 'what do you think about it/this?' Or it can be used as a statement in the negative:

> **Bù zěnme yàng** *Nothing special; It doesn't amount to much.*

The above is a useful expression to make an unfavourable remark on people or on a situation. To express an opinion more favourably but without enthusiasm you can use:

> **Má mǎ hū hū** *It's so so* (lit. horse horse tiger tiger).

Know the way

zhī [djr] **dao** [dow] *know; know of; realize; be aware of (a fact).* The second syllable is generally unstressed.

A compound expression whose literal meaning is 'know the way', Dao has the literal meaning of a 'road or pathway' and is used in expressions of means (i.e. way) to self-improvement such as the way of serving tea (**chá dào**), the way of writing (**shū dào**) and the way of the sword (**jiàn dao**; kendo in Japanese). Dao often appears in English as 'Tao' and is the founding concept of the Chinese body of philosophical and religious thought of Daoism.

> **Wǒ bù zhī daò** *I do not know (about that); I'm not sure.*
> **Wǒ zhī daò le** *I know. I see your point. I realize.*
> **Nǐ zhī dao ma?** *Do you know? Are you sure?*
> **Wǒ zhī dao tā huì lái** *I know that he will come.*
> **Nǐ zhī dao tā shì shuí ma?** *Do you know who he is?*

Note that *zhī dào* is used to know of or about a state of affairs. It is not used for knowing or being acquainted with people which requires the expression *rèn shi* (*shi* is unstressed) which can be used as follows:

> *Wǒ rèn shi nǐ ma?*   *Do I know you?*
> *Nǐ bú rèn shi wǒ ma?*   *Don't you know me?*
> *Wǒ men rèn shi*   *We know each other.*

As a noun, *rèn shi* is used to mean 'understanding', 'knowledge' and 'cognition'.

A well-known quotation from China's military classic the *Art of War* by Sun Zi goes:

> *Zhī jǐ zhī bǐ*   *Know your enemy and know yourself.*
> *Bǎi zhàn bú dài*   *In a hundred battles you will not be in danger.*

The first four words of this expression have entered common usage—if you know your opposition and know yourself you will never be defeated.

A useful expression to indicate uncertainty or reluctance to express an opinion:

> *Bù yí dìng*   *I'm not sure; Maybe; That's not certain.*
> *Yé xǔ*   *Perhaps.*

Similarly, to express an approximation you may use:

> *Chá bù duō*   *That's about* (right); *Close enough; More or less; So so.* (lit. difference not much)

This expression can be very constructively, as well as imaginatively, used but it may be frustrating to be on the receiving end of such an imprecise expression when something more direct is wanted. Its contextual usage is wide, for example:

> **Q:** *Zěmme yàng? Xíng ma?*   *How about it? Is it OK?*
> **A:** *Chà bu duō*   *More or less; So so.*

Another expression to indicate approximation which can also be used in a stand alone response is:

> *Dà gài*   *Probably; Likely.*
> **Q:** *Tā qī diǎn lái ma?*   *Will he come at 7 o'clock?*
> **A:** *Dà gài*   *Most likely.*

Proverb

Zhī zhě bù yán yán zhě bù zhī

Those that speak do not know and those that know do not speak.

zhī	know
zhě	those
bù yán	not speak
yán zhě	those who speak
bù zhī	not know

A well known quotation about knowledge from the Daoist classic the *Dao De Jing* (Chapter 56). The authorship is attributed to Lao Zi (born 604 BC) the reputed founder of Daoism who taught that men should not strive, but should pursue a course of inaction because things will come to a successful conclusion without effort.

The often enigmatic language of the *Dao De Jing* has made it the most frequently translated of all classical

Chinese texts. A number of its enigmatic sayings are still quoted today in ordinary conversation including the well known opening lines:

> ***Dào kě dào, fēi cháng dào; míng kě míng, fēi cháng míng***
> *The Dao that can be expressed is not the eternal Dao; The name that can be named is not the eternal name.*
>
> (Richard Wilhelm trans.)

This quintessential expression of the inherent ambiguity of language contrasts with the Confucian conviction that insists on 'correct names' (***zhèng míng***). These fundamentally contrasting views continue to inform behaviour in China today—not least of all in international relations, politics and business. Aspects of the behaviour and conduct of Chinese you meet may be more influenced by one or the other.

16

What is this?

Zhè shì shénme?

zhè [jay]   *this* (one here)

In northern China there is a strong 'r' sound at the end of many syllables. In this case *zhè* is pronounced 'zhr'. It makes no difference to the meaning. Pronounce whatever comes most easily. The complementary expression is *nèi* [nah/nar], *that* (one there). These expressions are most often heard as:

> *Zhè ge*   *This* (one).
> *Nèi ge*   *That* (one).

Zhè ge is also often heard repeated as a sound to express hesitation or uncertainty—the equivalent of 'um' in English. Note that the *ge* is unstressed.

> *Zhè ge hén hǎo*   *This one is good.*
> *Nèi ge bù hǎo*   *That one is not good.*
> *Zhè ge rén shì wǒ de péng you*   *This person is my friend.*
> *Nèi ge rén hěn kè qi*   *That person is very polite.*

Grammar note

'The' as a definite article does not exist in Chinese. If you need to be specific about a particular object the words for 'this' and 'that' are often used. Usually when 'the' would be used in English, *zhè/nèi* will be used in Chinese, though where articles always appear in English they are most often left unexpressed in Chinese:

> **Tiān qì hén hǎo**   *The weather is fine.*
> **Zhè li de rén hěn yóu hǎo**   *The people here are friendly.*

Related expressions

> **zhè li**   *here*
> **zhè ge dì fang**   *this place*
> **nèi li**   *there* (over there, i.e. away from the speaker)
> **nèi ge dì fang**   *that place* (there)
> **Zhè ge dì fang bú cuò**   *This place is pretty good.*
> **Nèi ge dì fang wǒ bù zhī dào**   *I don't know about that place.*
> **Nèi ge dì fang wǒ méi qù**   *I've never been there.*
> **Zhè shì shénme dì fang?**   *What place is this?*

Geography

Fāng (lit. square) has an important use in defining the directions: *dōng* (east), *nán* (south), *xī* (west), *běi* (north). Note that this is the usual order in which the directions (*fāng xiàng*) are spoken of in conversation. This use of *fāng* also creates:

> *dōng fāng*   east, the East; eastern
> *nán fāng*   south; southern
> *xī fāng*   west, the West/Occident; western
> *běi fāng*   north, northern

As a visitor to China you may be the subject of the following expression:

> *Tā men shì xī fāng rén*   They are 'Westerners.'

This usually refers to people who are European, North American or from other other Western, usually English speaking, countries.

Cultural note

The number of expressions used to refer to Europeans in China reflects the mixed history of China's encounter with the West. From the time of Marco Polo's visit in the 13th century (Yuan Dynasty) there followed an array of medieval friars, merchants, officials and assorted adventurers so that by the 1930s there were almost 100 000 foreigners in Shanghai alone.

Remarks concerning physical appearance, for example *dà bí zi*, 'big nose' and *hóng máo zi*, 'red hairy ones', have proved to be enduring. Use of the word *yáng* in its meaning of 'ocean' has been used to refer to many products that were foreign in origin and in the expression *yáng guǐ zi*, 'foreign devils'. This is still used—when not expected to be overheard!

In China the defining geographical distinction between north and south is the Yang tze River (*yáng zi jiāng*) and you will notice expressions such as:

běi fāng rén   northerner
nán fāng rén   southerner
Tā shì nán fang rén   *He is from the south (of China).*

Interestingly enough there is no comparable usage of east and west within China. This reflects the fact that the majority of Han Chinese live on the fertile and agriculturally prosperous east coast, and most of the minority groups live in the western regions.

There may be occasions when it may be necessary to point out:

Wǒ men de fāng xiàng cuò le   *Our direction is wrong.*

This may be addressed to a taxi driver who appears to be taking a circuitous route; as well as to your official interlocutor when discussions have gone off the rails.

Proverb

Sì miàn chū gē

In desperate straights;
besieged on all sides;
utterly isolated.

sì	four
miàn	side
chū	ancient kingdom
gē	song

In the final battle for the empire after the fall of the Qin dynasty, the leader of the Chu armies heard the songs of

Chu in the camp of the opposing forces and realized his troops had deserted him. Admitting defeat, he killed his horse and his concubine before killing himself.

The story was made familiar by the film *Farewell My Concubine*. The expression means to be surrounded on all sides with no hope of rescue and can be used to refer to any hopeless situation.

17

Let me think about it
Ràng wŏ xiăng yì xiăng

ràng [r + h<u>ung</u>]   *allow; permit; let*
  Ràng wŏ kàn   *Let me see.*
  Ràng tā lái   *Let him come.*
  ráng bù   *to concede; compromise; back down*
  Wŏ bù ràng bù   *I won't back down; compromise.*

Cultural note
Ràng is another word that bears a heavy cultural load in Chinese. It expresses a far reaching concept whose importance is expressed in the original meaning of 'yield' or 'give way' that appealed particularly to the Daoists. By extension the word means to show restraint and (display) humility—behaviour that was highly esteemed in traditional China and still finds a place in expressions of common courtesy in China today. A saying has it 'to yield does not mean that I am weak, but that I am under self-restraint and leave blustering to others'. It is also the word that is used in road signs today for give way. There is something of the idea of *réculer pour mieux sauter* (i.e. one step back and two steps forward) in the

extended significance of the word. A strategic negotiating tactic the world over.

xiǎng *think about; suppose/guess*
  Wó xiǎng shì *I guess so.* (It is the case.)
  Wó xiǎng tā bù lái *I suppose he is not coming.*
  Wǔ hén xiǎng tā *I miss him/her a lot.*
  Ní xiǎng tā ma? *Do you miss her/him?*
  Wǒ yì diǎn bù xiǎng tā *I do not miss him/her/ it at all.*

Related expressions

  xiǎng bú dào *unexpected; I never thought of that*
  Méi xiǎng dào! *Fancy that!*
  xiǎng jiā *be homesick* (lit. think family)
  Tā hén xiǎng jiā *He/she is homesick.*
  xiǎng yì [ee] **xiǎng** *have a think* (about something)

This construction—**xiǎng yì xiǎng**—is frequently encountered and is created by repeating the verb separated by the sound **yi** (i.e. one). It suggests that an action takes place for a short period of time. It appears in expressions such as:

  Ní xiǎng yì xiǎng *Have a think about it.*
  Kàn yì kàn *Have a look.*
  Děng yì děng *Wait a moment.*
  Qíng ni děng yì děng *Please wait a moment.*

shì yí shì   have a try; have a shot at
Zǒu yì zǒu   Take (or go for) a walk.

As noted in Chapter 11, *xiǎng* can be used to politely express an intention and when used in this situation can express the following:

Wó xiǎng kàn yí kàn   I would like to take a look.
Wó xiǎng shì yí shì   I would like to have a try.
Wó xiáng zǒu yì zǒu   I would like to take a walk.

More related expressions

xiāng xìn   to believe; trust
   Wǒ xiāng xìn nǐ   I believe/trust you.
Wǒ bú xìn   I don't believe it.
Wǒ xiāng xìn tā shì yī ge hǎo rén   I believe he is a good person.
Nǐ xiāng xìn tā hùi lái ma?   Do you believe that he will come?

Cultural note

Trust (*xìn*) is another of the Five Constant (*wǔ cháng*) Confucian virtues that provide useful insights into the Chinese ethical system—which places a high premium on secular humanism rather than an omnipotent transcendent being. The virtues that are displayed by the perfect person (and quoted in this order) are:

   rén   benevolence
   yí   uprightness of mind; duty to one's neighbour
   lǐ   propriety in demeanour

> *zhī* knowledge; wisdom
> *xìn* good faith; trustworthiness

Xìn is associated with ideas of truth, sincerity, confidence and fidelity. Related expressions include:

xìn rèn trust/have confidence in someone's ability or character
   Nǐ bù xín rèn wǒ ma? Don't you trust me?
xìn xīn confidence; faith
   Wó yǒu xìn xīn I am confident.
   Xìn xīn bú dà I don't have much confidence in it.
xín yì good faith
xìn yǎng belief; conviction
xín lài trust; count on; have faith in
   Wǒ men ké yǐ xín lài tā We can have faith in/rely on him.
mí [mee] confused; lost; fascinated by
mí xìn superstition; be superstitious
   Tā hěn mí xìn She/he is superstitious.
qíu mí football fan
xì mí opera fan

Proverb

Tiān xià wéi gōng
The world belongs to everyone.

tiān sky; heaven
xià under
wéi is
gōng public; common

As everything under heaven (a common expression from classical language to refer to everything in the world) is considered to be public property so everyone has a responsibility to be concerned with public affairs. Originally a line from the Confucian classic *Book of Rites* (**Li Ji**) it was later quoted by Sun Yat Sen (1866–1925) to express his concept of people's rights and subsequently became more widely used.

As leader of the republican revolution that overthrew the Qing dynasty in 1911, Sun remains a revered figure in China where his grand mausoleum stands outside Nanjing. Sun's legacy and relevance is more controversial for Taiwan as it seeks to distinguish its own identity.

18

Heaven's above!

Lǎo tiān yé!

Lǎo tiān yé is an expression that literally means 'the old man in the sky'. It is used colloquially as an exclamation of surprise to mean 'my goodness!', 'good gracious', 'my God!'. As popular belief has it *lǎo tiān yǒu yán* (Heaven has eyes)—Heaven sees all and will protect the good and punish the wicked.

Yé ye by itself is the term of direct address for one's paternal grandfather or a respectful but informal term of address to a very elderly man. *Lǎo yé ye* can have the meaning of great-grandfather. *Lǎo ye* was once used as a respectful term of address by a servant to a master but it is now more often used sarcastically.

An equally useful all-purpose exclamation that makes use of similar terminology is:

Tiān a!   *Good heavens; my God!*
  Wǒ de tiān a!   *Oh, my God!* (the 'a' represents a sound with no inherent meaning).

Cultural note

Expressions of frustration and (mild) rebuke are a useful addition to your vocabulary and can enhance expressiveness. It is important to bear in mind that such expressions from a foreign speaker need to be carefully considered. They can be easily misunderstood and just as easily cross the bounds of both good taste and the common courtesy that is always expected of the visitor as much as the long-term foreign resident. Meeting expectations in regard to behaviour are of paramount consideration in getting the most out of relationships in China. The matter of face—giving and saving—has a long established place in defining interpersonal relationships in China and needs to be kept in mind when expressing frustration. It's all best done with a smile on your face—whatever is in your mind!

The selection of expressions that follow is provided from among the great variety from which to choose that enliven daily exchange between Chinese people.

In relation to face:

> **lián**   *face; personal honour; social prestige*
>> **Bú yào lián**   *Shameless! What a nerve!*
>> **diū lián**   *lose face; be disgraced*
>> **Zhēn/tài diū lián**   *Too shameful; That's a real loss of face.*

The following expressions can be used in a wide variety of situations and, if used with appropriate discretion, can be guaranteed to liven up flagging conversation—without overstepping the mark. The creative speaker should have fun experimenting with these expressions.

shǎ   *be silly; foolish; stupid; muddleheaded*
   Nǐ bié shǎ   *Don't be silly; foolish.*
Shǎ guā/zi   *What a fool; blockhead; simpleton!* (lit. stupid melon)
   Tā shì ge shǎ guā   *He's a fool!*
Yào mìng   *What a nuisance!* (lit. drive someone to death)
Hú shuō bā daò   *Nonsense!*
Bú xiàng huà   *That's outrageous! Shocking!*
Běn dàn   *What a fool; half-wit! Idiot!* (lit. stupid egg)
Zhēn zāo gāo   *What a mess! That's a shame!*
Tā hén tǎo yàn   *He's annoying; disgusting; disagreeable.*
Huó gāi   *It serves you/him right; You deserve it.*
Hú li hú tu   *What a muddle head!*
Tā bù zhī tiān gāo dì hòu   *He's up himself; has an exaggerated opinion of his own abilities* (lit. does not know heaven is high and the earth is thick).
Shén jīng bìng!   *He's/You're mad!* (lit. nervous illness)
bù sān bú sì   *shady; dubious* (lit. not three not four)
   bù sān bú sì de rén   *a shady character*

Proverb

Jiàn rén jiàn zhì

Different people have different views.

jiàn	see
rén	benevolence
jiàn	see
zhì	knowledge

This expression, meaning 'opinons differ' or 'there is no accounting for taste', literally means that the benevolent see it (i.e. the **dào**) and call it benevolent, while the wise see it and call it wisdom. It occurs in the *I Ching* or *Book of Changes* (**yì jīng**), universally recognised as one of the most profound and obscure of the Confucian canonical texts among which it occupies foremost place.

It is a comprehensive system of cosmology elaborated in terms of the principles of Yin and Yang, as well as a book of divination still used by fortune tellers today. Its basic text, which is 3000 years old, explains each of the 64 hexgrams (sets of six broken and unbroken lines) while the commentary on their metaphysical significance is traditionally attributed to Confucius.

The psychological insights of this classic attracted the attention of Carl Jung who called it a 'great and singular book'. Attracted to the challenge it posed to the rationalist Western preoccupation with causality as an explanation for events, he observed (in his Foreword to Richard Wilhelm's masterful translation), 'While the Western mind carefully sifts, weighs, selects, classifies, isolates, the Chinese picture of the moment encompasses everything down to the minutest nonsensical detail, because all of the ingredients make up the observed moment.' A conversation about the *I Ching* can lead just about anywhere.

19

Climb higher see further
Gèng shàng yī céng lóu

The pervasive use of literary expression in common spoken language provides insights into some of the enduring ideals and values that continue to find favour in China, and represents a fascinating interaction of literary and popular culture. The variety of proverbial and cultural expressions, if used appropriately, can *huà lǒng diǎn jīng*—'bring the picture of a dragon to life by painting in the pupils of the eyes' (i.e. adding just the right word or phrase in the right place to make a point). The right saying at the right time can be guaranteed to stimulate appreciative responses—and hopefully some further cultural exchange and understanding. To the enduring surprise and delight of his hosts during Richard Nixon's visit to China in February 1972, he used a quotation from a 1963 poem written by Chairman Mao:

> *Yī wàn nián tài jiǔ, zhǐ zhēng zhāo xī*
> *Ten thousand years are too long, sieze the day, seize the hour.*

The lines are well known by a generation of Chinese still fascinated (and still not a little amazed) by this initial blossoming of US–PRC relations. The context reveals the appropriateness of the quotation:

> So many deeds cry out to be done,
> And always urgently;
> The world rolls on,
> Time passes.
> Ten thousand years are too long,
> Seize the day, seize the hour.

Poetic expressions with their origins in an oral tradition are short and easy to remember and can be used to maximum effect as stand alone expressions without the need for more complex language around them.

It should come as no surprise that China's vast classical literature, its poetry in particular, provides a wealth of expressions in proverbial sayings and quotations. So well-committed to memory are these works that a few words (no matter how badly pronounced) will be understood.

Gèng shàng yī céng lóu is the final line from a Tang poem by Wang Zhi Yuan (688–742), *Ascending the Crane Tower* (*Deng he que lou*):

> *Bái rì yī shān jìn*   *The bright sun against the mountains*
> *Huáng hé rù hǎi liú*   *The Yellow River entering the sea*
> *Yù qióng qiān lǐ mù*   *To command a vista of a thousand*
>   *miles*
> *Gèng shàng yī céng lóu*   *Climb up one storey higher*

The full poem gives a taste for how the poetic language works and how the sense of the allusion informs its everyday usage. Chinese children learn such easy works from the classical canon that make such allusions familiar to most Chinese. The final line is frequently quoted to indicate the advantages to be gained by higher achievement and in the context of the whole poem refers to the more expansive view that is gained by climbing to a higher level of a pagoda. See an example of the usage of this expression at page 104. The use of such sayings reveals a cultural preference for indirect expression that draws on the power of imaginative suggestion in its underlying sensibility.

The written language abounds in references from literature and history that present major challenges to the mastery of the language by native speakers and foreign students alike. Another eminently quotable stanza from the *Spring Night's Happy Rain* (**Chun ye xi yu**) poem by Du Fu (712–770), considered by many to be China's greatest classical poet:

> **Háo yǔ zhī shí jié**   *Timely rain falls in the right season*
> **Dāng chūn nǎi fā shēng**   *Spring is just when it occurs*
> **Suí fēng qiǎn rù yè**   *Blown by wind in the depths of night*
> **Rùn wù xì wú shēng**   *Soaking things gently in silence.*

The first line can be quoted to indicate the occurrence of an opportune event, while the last line can be used to refer to anything positive that occurs subtly without undue attention.

The following example can be used when in need of a phrase to express the idea that there are hopeful signs that a situation can be retrieved. Lines of the poem *Mountain Excursion to West Village* (*you shan xi cun*) by the Song Dynasty patriotic poet, official and history writer Lu You (1125–1210) allude to coming across a village after being lost in the mountains:

> *Shān chóng shuǐ fù yí wú lù*   Midst mountains and rivers
> we fear the way is lost
> *Liú àn huā míng yòu yī cūn*   With dark willows and
> bright flowers appears
> another village.

The words *liú àn huā míng* (lit. willows dark flowers bright) are sufficient to indicate the reference and suggest that bright new prospects have opened up when least expected and things are back on track.

The last two lines of the well known quatrain *Spring Dawn* (*chun xiao*) by Meng Hao Ran (689–740) have been used to discreetly allude to the darkest days of the Cultural Revolution:

> *Yè lái fēng yǔ shēng*   Nightfall brings the clamour of wind
> and rain
> *Huā luò zhī duō shǎo*   And fallen flowers who knows
> how many?

The following are a selection of well known idiomatic sayings that will indicate a more than passing acquaintance with the language. Favourites can be usefully memorized as an aid to distinguishing the tonal patterns of the language. Nevertheless these sayings are so well known that incorrect tones will be no obstacle to conveying the intended meaning.

Huó dào lǎo xué dào lǎo *You're never too old to learn* (lit. live 'til old age/study 'til old age).

Bú dào huáng hé xīn bù sǐ *Never say die* (lit. not reach Yellow River/heart not die).

Qí hú nán xià *Riding the tiger* (lit. riding tiger difficult dismount).

Rù xiāng suí sú *When in Rome...* (lit. enter village follow custom).

Tiān bú pà/ dì bú pà *Fearless and courageous* (lit. heaven not fear/earth not fear). The original quote continues to say 'the only thing to be feared is a foreign devil speaking Chinese!'

Xīn zhào bù xuān *Inscrutable* (lit. heart clear not announce).

Xīn zhōng yǒu shù *Know the score* (lit. heart middle has number).

Bǎi fā bǎi zhòng *Successful every time* (lit. one hundred aims one hundred strikes).

Yì jǔ liǎng dé *Kill two birds with one stone* (lit. one lift two receive).

Shùn qí zì rán *Go with the flow* (lit. follow it own nature).

Sān rén xíng/ bì yǒu wǒ shī *Learn from everyone* (lit. three persons together walk/must have my teacher).

Gù zhǎng nán míng *It takes two to tango* (lit. single hand difficult clap).

Proverb

Jiǎ zuò zhēn shí zhēn yì jiǎ
When false is true, truth is also false.

jiǎ	false
zuò	make
zhēn	true
shí	time
yì	also

This is the first line of a well known couplet that appears in the opening chapter of China's greatest classical novel, written in the eighteenth-century, *The Dream of the Red Chamber* (**Hóng loú mèng**). While few people these days will have read all its 120 chapters (some two and a half thousand pages in English translation) which chart the glory and decline of the illustrious Jia family, everyone knows of the heir of the family Jia Bao Yu and his doomed romance with Lin Dai Yu, two of the most well-known characters in all Chinese literature.

The essentially tragic theme affirms a Buddhist belief in a supernatural order that is made explicit in the associated line of the couplet: *wú wéi yǒu chù yǒu huán wú*   *when nothing beomes something, something also becomes nothing*. The lines work as a series of puns in Chinese that can also mean:

Truth becomes fiction when the fiction's true;
Real becomes unreal when then unreal's real.

Find the meaning where you will.

20

Ladies and Gentlemen!
Xiān shēng men, nǚ shì men

Once you have mastered Chinese pinyin spelling and the basics of Chinese grammar you are already prepared for more ambitious use of the spoken language in the form of a formal speech. A short formal speech in Chinese is far from the daunting prospect that it may appear. Reading from a prepared text in pinyin will achieve the desired end.

Formal spoken language in Chinese is characterized by highly formulaic structural patterns that draw heavily on the classical language in its use of regular fixed expressions often made up of a series of four, five or six characters. The content of formal remarks usually cover a narrow range of conventional expressions concerning past experience, the present situation and hopes for the future. The following provide a sample of such language that may be usefully incorporated into an occasion calling for formal remarks. A formal speech is the opportunity to surprise and delight and, above all, entertain your hosts.

The following provides language that can be used in a formal speech. The sample of official speech exposes the beginner to the use of more sophisticated vocabulary that can also be used in more ambitious conversation. Minor amendments may make the following appropriate to a specific occasion. The sentiments expressed are those frequently heard on formal occasions as part of official intercourse. It is important to address remarks to the official guests in the order of known seniority. A list of official titles is at Appendix A. For ease of expression '/' have been added where pauses may occur most naturally.

Xiān shēng men / nǔ shì men   *Ladies and Gentlemen*

Wǒ hěn róng xìng / cān jīa / jīn tiān de / dà huì   *I am very honoured to attend this conference today.*
   róng xìng   *be honoured* (used in polite statements)
   cān jīa   *join in; participate in; take part; attend*
   jīn tiān de   *today's* (*de* is used as a possessive particle)
   huì yì   *meeting*
   dà huì   *conference* (lit. big meeting)

Wó hěn gāo xìng / jiē dài / lái zì zhōng guó de / kè rén   *I am very pleased to host guests from China.*
   gāo xìng   *be happy; delighted*
   jiē dài   *receive; take care of* (guests)
   Lái zì   *to come from*
   Zhōng guó de   *Chinese* (i.e. China's)
   kè rén   *guest/s*

Kóng zǐ shuō / yǒu péng / zì yuán fāng lái / bú yì lè hū Confucius said, 'is it not a pleasure to have friends visit from afar?'

> *Kóng zǐ* Confucius
>
> *shuō* says
>
> *yǒu péng* there are friends
>
> *zì yuán fāng lái* from distant place come
>
> *bú yì lè hū* extremely; awfully (used as an exclamation).

(Fore more detail on this quotation, see the proverb on page 36.)

Wǒ dài biǎo…duì wǒ men / zhōng guó guī bīn / biǎo shì / rè liè huān yíng On behalf of…I wish to extend a warm welcome to our honoured guests from China.

> *Dài biǎo* represent
>
> *Duì wǒ men* towards our
>
> *Guī bīn* honoured guests
>
> *Biǎo shì* express; signify; make clear
>
> *Rè liè* warm; heartfelt
>
> *Huān yíng* welcome

Zhōng guó rén mín / qín láo / chuàng yè / jiàn shè jiā yuán / tuán jié fèn dòu de / jīng shén / jǔ shī wén míng The Chinese people are renowned for their diligence and enterprising industriousness as well as their unity and hard working spirit.

> *rén mín* people
>
> *qín láo* hard working
>
> *chuàng yè* enterprising

jiàn shè build; develop; construct

jiā yuán home and garden

tuán jié be united

fèn dòu struggle hard

jīng shén spirit

jǔ shì wén míng renowned (lit. all world heard clear)

Zhōng guó / duì shì jiè wén míng / yóu jǔ dà de / gōng xiàn China has made a great contribution to world civilization.

duì in regard to

shì jiè world

wén míng civilization

jǔ dà great; large

gōng xiàn contribution

Guò qù / rú cǐ This was the case in the past.

guò qù past

rú cǐ like this

Jīn tiān / hái jì chéng / hé / fā zhǎn / zhè yōu liáng / chuán tóng This fine tradition is being continued and developed today.

hái still; again

jì chéng inherit; continue; carry on

hé and

fā zhǎn develop; expand

zhè (ge) *this* (one)

yōu liáng fine; hallowed

chuán tóng tradition

Wǒ zài zhōng guó / qīn yǎn kàn dào le / xiàn dài zhōng guó de / gǎi gé kāi fàng zhèng cè / duì zhōng guó fā zhǎn de / jǔ dà gòng xiàn   I have seen in China with my own eyes the great contributions to China's development that has been made by contemporary China's present reform policies.

> *zài*   to be at; in
>
> *qīn yǎn*   (my) own eyes
>
> *kàn dào*   be seen; saw
>
> *xiàn dài*   present; contemporary
>
> *gǎi gé*   reform
>
> *kāi fàng*   open; broad-minded
>
> *zhèng cè*   policy

Wǒ zhù / zhōng guó de fā zhǎn / jiàn shè / gèng shàng yī céng lóu   Let me express the hope that China's development will reach even greater heights!

> *Zhù*   (I) wish
>
> *Gèng shàng yī céng lóu*   Climb up one storey higher
> (See Chapter 19 for meaning)

Zhōng guó de rén / duì wǒ guó / kāi fā jiàn shè / yǒu zhe / jī jí de gòng xiàn   Chinese people have made positive contributions to the development of my country.

> *duì*   in relation to
>
> *kāi fā*   opening
>
> *yǒu zhe*   having; have
>
> *jī jí*   positive
>
> *gòng xiàn*   contribution

Zài wǒ guó / huá rén de cōng míng / cái zhì / zhuān yè jì néng / shāng mào huó dòng / tuì dòng le / wǒ guó de / fán róng / zēng jiā le / wǒ guó de / guó jí jìng zhēng lì The intelligence, wisdom, expertise and business activities of people of Chinese descent in our country have promoted our prosperity and increased our international competitiveness.

> *huá rén* people of Chinese descent (i.e. not citizens of China)
>
> *cōng míng* intelligent; smart
>
> *cái zhì* talent; ability
>
> *zhuān yè* expert(ise)
>
> *jì néng* skill; talent
>
> *shāng mào* commerce and trade
>
> *huó dòng* activity
>
> *tuì dòng* promote; further
>
> *fán róng* prosperity
>
> *zēng jiā* increase
>
> *guó jí* international
>
> *jìng zhēng lì* competitiveness

Duì cǐ / wó biǎo shì / gòng zhù / hé / jīng yì For this I wish to express respect and congratulations!

> *duì cǐ* in relation to this
>
> *gòng zhù* congratulation; felicitation
>
> *hé* and
>
> *jìng yì* respect; reverence

Wŏ men / hé zhōng guó / yí yŏu / jĭ shí nián de / guān xì   Our relationship with China is over several decades long.

   yí yŏu   *already has*
   jĭ shí   *several decades*
   nián   *year*
   guān xì   *relations; relationship*

Zhè shì wŏ / dì…cí / lái zhōng guó / yí cì / bĭ yí cì / biàn huà / dà   This is my (**number**) visit to China; there are greater changes on each visit.

   dì…cì   *…th* (indicating e.g. the 4th time i.e. *dì sì cì*)
   yí cì bĭ yí cì   *one time compared to one time*
   biàn huà   *change; transformation*
   dà   *very big; large*

Wŏ men / gōng tóng de / nŭ lì / tuī dòng le / wŏ men de / yóu hăo / hé zuò guān xì de / fā zhăn   Our common efforts have promoted the development of our friendly cooperative relations.

   gōng tóng   *general, common; jointly, together*
   nŭ lì   *make efforts; strive*
   yóu hăo   *friendship*
   hé zuò   *cooperation*

Zhōng guó / shì wŏ men de / yí gè / zhòng yào / máo yì huŏ bàn   China is one of our important trading partners.

   yí gè   *one* (of)
   zhòng yào   *important*
   máo yì   *trade*
   huŏ bàn   *partner*

Duì / wǒ men de / yóu hǎo hé zuò de / fā zhǎn / wó biǎo shì / rè liè zhù hè I wish to extend my warm congratulations to the growth of our friendship and cooperation!

> *duì* in regard to
> *wǒ men de* our
> *yóu hǎo* friendship; friendly
> *hé zuò* cooperation
> *fā zhǎn* development; growth
> *biǎo shì* express; indicate
> *rè liè zhù hè* warm congratuation/s

Wǒ men / hé / zhōng guó de / jiāo wǎng / zēng zhǎng / hěn kuài The exchange beween us and China has increased quickly.

> *jiāo wǎng* exchange; intercourse
> *zēng zhǎng* increase
> *hěn kuài* very fast

Yuè lái / yuè duō de / zhōng guó rén / lái wǒ guó / lǚ yóu More and more Chinese people are visiting our country as tourists.

> *yuè lái yuè duō* the more
> *lǚ yóu* travel (as a tourist)

Wǒ guó / shì yí gè / tuán jié / hé xié de / duō yuán wén huà / guó jiā We are a united and harmonious multicultural country.

> *tuán jié* unite(d)
> *hé xié* harmonious
> *duō yuán wén huà* multicultural
> *guó jiā* country; nation

Gè mín zǔ / rén mín / bāo kuò / huá rén / tuán jié hé zuò / gòng tóng nǔ lì / fēng fù le / wǒ guó wén huà / cū jìn le / wǒ guó de / fán róng Every nationality including those of Chinese descent are united in cooperation to make common efforts to enrich our culture and develop our prosperity.

> *gè*   each
> *mín zǔ*   nationality; race
> *bào kuò*   include; comprise
> *fēng fù*   (make) prosperous
> *wén huà*   culture
> *cù jìn*   promote; enhance
> *fán róng*   be prosperous; flourishing

Wǒ xī wàng / jīn tiān de / dà huì / jiāng cù jìn / jīng jì de / fā zhǎn / dài dòng / guó jí jiāo liú / tuī jìn / wǒ men de / yǒu yì I hope today's conference will further promote economic prosperity, enhance international exchange and further our friendship.

> *xī wàng*   hope
> *jiāng*   will
> *jīng jì*   economics
> *dài dòng*   enhance (lit. pull along)
> *jiāo liú*   exchange
> *tuī jìn*   promote (lit. push forward)

Wǒ men de / yǒu hǎo / hé zuò de / qián jǐng / guǎng kuò There are broad prospects for our friendly cooperation.

> *qián jǐng*   prospect
> *guǎng kuò*   broad; expansive; wide; vast

Ràng wǒ men / wèi wǒ men de / yǒu yì / gòng tóng nǔ lì   Let us strive together for the sake of our friendship.
  ràng   let
  wèi   for (the benefit of)

Hǎi nèi cún zhī jǐ tiān yǎ ruò bǐ lín   Good friends in distant lands make us all neighbours.
  hǎi nèi   within the seas
  cún   are; exist
  zhī jǐ   friends; intimates
  tiān yǎ   the edge of the world
  ruò   to be like
  bǐ lín   neighbour

This is a frequently used quotation to express sentiments concerning how friendship can overcome distance. A quotation from the Tang poet Wang Bo (648–675) subsequently made more well known when used by Mao Ze Dong to describe the close relationship between China and Albania in the 1960s.

And finally:

Xiè xie dà jiā   thank you everyone
dà jiā   everyone

21

A Beginner's Vocabulary for Adults

This vocabulary selection is designed to complement the previous lessons and provide more language which will offer you more opportunities to express thoughts, opinions and feelings in a variety of situations. With an emphasis on self-expression it is not specifically designed to solicit information or otherwise engage in dialogue, though any interest in the language and any displayed ability can nevertheless be guaranteed to engage most people in further exchanges.

Though technical language and questions which will solicit complex responses have been avoided (as they are beyond the scope of the beginner), the selected vocabulary is a handy introduction to simple but useful expressions that highlight the basic structural and linguistic working features of Mandarin. This can provide a starting point from which the interested beginner can further explore the vast continent of the Chinese language.

The words and phrases featured in this list include instances where two falling tones appear together (i.e. the first will become a rising tone) as well as when two third tones appear together (i.e. the first is generally pronounced as a rising tone.)

A

about; **almost**; more or less   *chà bù duō*
    We are almost there.   *Wǒ men chà bù duō dào le.*
    How about it?   *Zěnme yàng?*

absolutely; definitely   *jué duì*
    He'll definitely come.   *Tā jué duì lái.*
    You're absolutely right.   *Nǐ jué duì méi cuò.*

by **accident**; by chance   *ǒu rán*
    We met by accident.   *Wǒ men ǒu rán pèng shang le.*

accurate   *zhèng què*
    Completely correct.   *Wán quán zhèng què.*

active (social/political life)   *huó yuè*
    She's very active (socially).   *Tā hěn huó yuè.*

advance (progress)   *jìn bù*
    He's made a lot of progress.   *Tā jìn bù hěn dà.*

agree   *dā ying*
    Did he agree?   *Tā dā ying le ma?*
    Have you agreed?   *Dā yīng le ma?*

I **agree** with whatever you have suggested.   *shénme dōu ké yǐ*

aim; goal   *mù dì*
    We have the same aim.   *Wǒ men de mù dì shì yí yàng de.*

angry   *shēng qì*
    Don't be angry.   *Bié shēng qì.*
    Why are you angry?   *Nǐ wèi shénme shēng qì?*

Another cup please. *Qǐng zài lái yì bēi.*

another; other (besides this one) *qí tā de*

Do you have another one? *Yǒu qí tā de ma?*

More; additional; another *bié de*

anxious *zháo jí*

Don't be anxious. *Bié zháo jí.*

Anything goes; whatever; I agree with whatever you have suggested. *shénme dōu ké yǐ*

appreciate *xīn shǎng*

I appreciate him. *Wó hěn xīn shǎng tā.*

approach; method *fǎ zi*

That's a good approach. *fǎ zi hén hǎo.*

assistant *zhù shǒu*

This is my assistant. *Tā shì wǒ de zhù shǒu.*

pay **attention** *zhù yì*

(to have) **authority** *fù zé rèn*

Who is in authority? *Shuí fù zé rèn?*

awful; bad *hěn huài*

He's an awful person. *Tā hěn huài.*

That's an awful shame. *Zhēn zāo gāo.*

He's awfully boring. *Tā zhēn wú liáo.*

B

bad *huài; bù hǎo*

The weather is bad. *Tiān qì hěn huài.*

He has a bad temper. *Tā de pí qi hěn huài.*

feel bad; uncomfortable *jué de bù shū fu*

feel sad; sorry *nán guò*

I feel sorry (about that)   *wó hĕn nán guò*

taste bad   *bù hăo chī*

bad luck   *dăo méi*

That's bad luck.   *Zhēn dăo méi.*

To be **baffled**, puzzled; unable to make head nor tail of
something   *Mò míng qí miào*

banquet   *yàn huì*

be a **bargain**; cheap   *pián yì*

able to **bear**; stand   *shòu de liăo*

Can you bear it?   *Nĭ shòu de liăo ma?*

beautiful   *hăo; mĕi; hăo kàn; hăo tīng*

I beg your pardon.   *Duì bu qĭ.*

benefit   *hăo chù*

That's not beneficial.   *Méi yóu hăo chù.*

best   *zuì hăo*

best (looking)   *zuì hăo kàn*

bible   *shèng jīng*

big   *dà*

big shot; big wig   *dà rén wù*

What's the big idea!; What does that mean?   *Shénme
yì si!*

big hearted   *qì liang dà*

birds of a feather   *wù yĭ leì jù*

Were you **born** in...?   *Nĭ shì...rén ma?*

bother; care about   *gŭan*

don't bother me   *bié gŭan wŏ*

breakfast   *zăo cān*

(Please) **bring** a glass of water.   *(Qíng) dào yì bēi shuĭ.*

broken   *huài le*

Be busy *máng*

I'm busy. *Wó hĕn máng.*

Not so busy *bù máng*

No longer be busy *bù máng le*

Have (free) time *yŏu kòng*

C

What shall I **call** her? *Wŏ jiào tā shénme?*

What do you call this in Chinese? *Zhōng wén zhè jiào shénme?*

That was a close call! *Zhēn xiăn!*

calm (disposition) *wĕn zhòng*

Keep **calm**. *Bié huāng.*

Can I help you? *Wŏ néng bāng máng ma?*

I can do it! *Wŏ huì le!*

I can't understand. *Wŏ bù dŏng.*

Take **care** of yourself (usually said on parting) *Duō duō băo zhòng.*

Be careful!; Look out! *Xiăo xīn!*

Listen carefully *Zhù yì tīng.*

I don't care. *Wŏ bú zài hu.*

carry weight/authority *yŏu lì liang*

I didn't **catch** his name. *Wŏ méi tīng qīng chu tā de míng zi.*

cause *yuán yīn*

certainly *yí dìng*

Certainly not! *Dāng rán bú shì!*

chance (opportunity) *jī huì*

That's a good opportunity. *Hǎo jī huì.*

A good chance of success. *Yǒu chéng gōng de xī wàng.*

A good chance to win. *Yǒu yíng de xī wàng.*

There is a chance; maybe. *Yé xǔ.*

It may be possible. *Yé xǔ néng xíng.*

Don't take any chances. *Bié mào xiǎn.*

change *biàn*

He's changed. *Tā biàn le.*

Changed his mind. *Gǎi biàn le zhǔ yì.*

No charge (free). *Miǎn fèi.*

charming (scenery) *hén měi*

charming (person) *yǒu mèi li*

(to) **cheat**; deceive *piàn*

don't cheat/deceive *bié piàn rén*

I've been cheated *Wǒ shàng dàng le.*

Check! That's right. *Duì le.*

cheerful *kuài huó; gāo xìng*

child(ren) *xiǎo hái zi*

Do you have children? *Ní yóu xiǎo hái ma?*

fine looking children *hái zi hěn piào liang*

Keep your chin up! *Xiǎng kāi dian!*

choose *tiāo*

a good choice *tiāo hǎo le*

Christmas *shèng dàn*

Merry Christmas. *Shèng dàn kuài lè.*

civil; polite *yóu lǐ mào; kè qi*

classy; tasteful, be particular about *hén jiǎng jiu*

clear (sound; idea)   *qīng chu*
   It's not clear.   *Bù qīng chu.*
   Is it clear?   *Míng băi ma?; Dŏng ma?*
clever   *cōng ming*
close attention   *tè bié zhù yì*
cocky   *dé yì; zì dà*
Too **cold**? (e.g. the room)   *Tài lĕng ma?*
   He is cold (personality).   *Tā hén lĕng dàn*
Too **colourful.**   *Tài huā.*
not **comfortable**   *bù shū fu*
common; ordinary   *píng fán*
common sense   *cháng shì*
No **comparison.**   *Bù néng bĭ.*
compassionate   *cí bēi*
concern (involve); relevant   *yŏu guān xi*
   Does it concern me?   *Hé wó yŏu guān xi ma?*
conscience   *liáng xīn*
consider   *kăo lǜ*
   Let me consider it   *Ràng wó kăo lǜ·*
Control yourself.   *Bié huāng zhang.*
convenient   *fāng biàn*
Cool!   *Kù!*
cordial, polite   *kè qi*
That's **correct.**   *Duì.*
counterfeit; false; untrue   *jiă de*
Of course; Without doubt.   *Dāng rán.*
custom   *fēng sú*

D

Danger   *wéi xiăn*
    It's dangerous.   *Hĕn wéi xiăn.*
a **decent** person; well bred   *zhèng jing rén*
definitely; absolutely   *jué duì*
    definitely; without fail   *yí dìng*
    He'll definitely come.   *Tā jué duì lái.*
It **depends**; be in doubt.   *Bù yí dìng.*
difficult; not easy   *nán; bù róng yì*
disappoint   *shī wàng*
    I'm disappointed.   *Wŏ shī wàng le.*
do   *zùo*
    didn't do it well   *zuò de bù hăo*
    It will do you good.   *Duì nĭ yóu hăo chù.*
    Do (your) best.   *Nŭ lì.*
    Nothing to do with it.   *Méi yŏu guān xi.*
That's only a **dream**.   *Bú guò shì ge mèng.*
    Don't daydream.   *Bié hú xiăng.*
have a lot of **drive**/energy   *hén yŏu jīng shén*
dubious background (lit. come road not clear)   *lái lù
    bù míng*
dull (boring)   *méi yì si*
    dull (not intelligent)   *bù cōng ming*
    dull, monotonous; inflexible   *sí băn*
duty; responsibility   *zé rèn; yì wù*
    It's my duty.   *Wŏ fù zé rèn.*

E

eager to... *Hén xiǎng...*

easy *róng yì; bù nán*

> easy going *hěn hé qì; pí qi hén hǎo*
>
> I have no opinion/view; I'm easy. *Wǒ méi yǒu yì jiàn.*

Shall we **eat** now? (as a suggestion) *Xiàn zài chī fàn hǎo ba?*

> Please **eat** some more. *Qǐng zài chī yì diǎn.*

effect, benefit *hǎo chù*

> Is it beneficial? *Yóu hǎo chù ma?*

Do not put all your **eggs** in one basket. *Jiǎo tù sān kù* (lit. clever rabbit three burrows).

encourage *gǔ lì*

> I encourage him. *Wó gǔ lì tā.*

I hope you **enjoyed** dinner (host). *Dài màn de hěn* (lit. I've been a poor host).

especially good *tè bié hǎo*

(To) **exaggerate**; praise; You flatter me; I don't deserve such praise. *Tài kuā jiǎng le; kuā jiǎng*.

exception *lì wài*

> That's an exception. *Nèi shì lì wài.*

Can I **exchange** this? *Wǒ néng jiāo huàn ma?*

Please **excuse** my (bad) Chinese. *Qǐng yuán liàng wǒ gāng xué zhōng wén.*

expect *xī wàng*

> Don't expect too much. *Bié xī wàng tài duō.*

Please **explain**. *Qíng jiě shì.*

Thank you **very** much. *Fēi cháng xiè xie.*

> go to **extremes**; excessive *guò fèn*
>
> Don't overdo it. *Bié guò fèn.*

F

not **fair and square**   *bù gōng dào*
Words **fail** me   *wǒ shuō bù chū lái*
false/true   *jiǎ de/zhēn de*
famous   *yǒu míng*
  So **far** so good.   *Dào xiàn zài wèi zhǐ hái ké yǐ.*
fast   *kuài*
  The faster the better.   *Yuè kuài yuè hǎo.*
  fast friends   *jiāo qíng hěn shēn*
favourite   *zuì xǐ huān*
quite a **few**   *bù shǎo*
firm; conscientious   *rèn zhēn*
be **fit**/suitable   *hé shì*
follow (imitate)   *gēn tā xué*
  Do you follow me?   *Dǒng le ma?*
force   *mián qiǎng*
  not force (to)   *bù mián qiǎng*
  Don't force him to eat.   *Bù mián qiǎng tā chī fàn.*
forgive   *yuán liàng*
  Please forgive me.   *Qǐng yuán liàng wǒ.*
I **forgot**.   *Wǒ wàng le.*
  don't forget   *bié wàng*
  Forget it!   *Suàn le!*
free (no charge)   *miǎn fèi*
  I'm free now   *bù máng le; yǒu kòng*
  Feel free, as you like   *Suí biàn.*
A **friend** in need... (lit. in snow send coals)   *Xuě zhōng sòng tàn*
a lot of **fun**   *hǎo wán, yǒu yì si*
very **funny**   *zhēn hǎo xiào*
bright **future**   *qiān tú guāng míng*

G

generous; outgoing *dà fang*
You **go** first. *Nǐ xiān zǒu.*
good *hǎo*
    Good guess. *Cāi de hǎo.*
    Good natured *pí qi hǎo*
Gratitude is due him. *Yīng dāng gǎn ji tā.*
That's **great**! *Hǎo jí le!*
Guess! *Nǐ cāi cāi!*

H

habit *xí guàn*
    good habit *hǎo xí guàn*
    bad habit *bù hǎo xí guàn*
The situation is well **in hand**. *Yí qiè shùn lì.*
Happy Birthday. *Shēng rì kuài lè.*
It's **hard** to say. *Bù hǎo shuō; hěn nán shuō.*
head ache *tóu tòng*
    I have a headache. *Wǒ tóu tòng le.*
It's **over my head**! *Mò míng qí miào!*
His **heart** is in the right place. *Hǎo xīn rén.*
Heaven forbid! *Nèi kě bù xíng*
Get off your **high horse**! *Bié cuì le!*
hit it off well *yí qiè rú gù*
Hold your horses! *Bié zháo jí!*
Make yourself at **home**. *Bié kè qi.*
honest; frank *lǎo shí; chéng shí*
    to speak frankly *shuō shí huà*

It's too much of an **honour**. (in reply to a compliment or complimentary gesture, e.g. You speak Chinese very well; please take the seat of honour.) *Bù gǎn dāng.*

I **hope** so; I trust that is the case. *Wǒ xī wàng shì.*

Put the cart before the **horse**. *Qīng zhòng dǎo zhì; Qiān hòu dián dǎo.*

To be (and 'you are') a great **host**   *zhāo dài hěn zhōu dào*

hot blooded   *pí qì dà*

How are you going these days?   *Nǐ jìn lái zěnme yàng?*

We're only **human**.   *Rén fēi shèng xián, shú néng wú guò.*

I

That's a good **idea**.   *Hǎo zhù yì.*

It's not ideal.   *Bù lí xiǎng.*

ill; uncomfortable   *bù shū fu*

impossible   *bù kě néng*

Introduce   *jiè shào*

Allow me to present/introduce...   *Wǒ géi nǐ men jiè shào...*

J

Joke   *xiào hùa*

play a joke   *kāi wán xiào*

You're joking!   *Nǐ kāi wán xiào!*

Crack a joke   *shuō xiào hua*

He likes to crack jokes   *tā ài shuō xiào hua*

K

Are you **kidding**? *Nǐ kāi wán xiào ma?*

kind (generous) *hòu dào*

  kind hearted *xīn hǎo*

Kindness bears fruit/one good turn *Shàn yǒu shàn bào*

L

It's not a **laughing** matter. *Bù kě xiào.*

leave *zǒu*

  I ought to leave. *Wǒ gāi zǒu le.*

Leave me alone. *Bié guán wǒ.*

Don't **lie**; tell the truth. *Bié shuō jiǎ huà; Shuō shí huà.*

full of **life** *hén yǒu jīng shen; huó po*

We're in the same **line** (of business). *Wǒ men shì tóng háng.*

pay **lip service** (lit. hang out a sheep's head and sell dog meat) *guā yáng tóu mài gǒu ròu*

little, small *xiǎo*

  a little *yì diǎn*

  I can speak a little Chinese *wo hùi shūo yì diǎn zhōng wén*

look down on *kàn bù qǐ*

lose patience; be angry *shēng qì; fā pí qi*

Good **luck**; wish you success. *Zhù nǐ chéng gōng.*

Down on one's **luck**. *Dǎo méi.*

M

Makes no difference to me. *Wú suŏ wèi.*

I can **manage**. *Yŏu bàn fă.*

   manager *jīng lĭ*

(as a **matter**) of course *dāng rán*

   A matter of opinion (lit. each person's view is not the
      same) *gè rén kàn fă bù tóng*

   It doesn't matter. *Méi yŏu guān xi.*

May I? *Wó ké yĭ ma?*

may as well *gān cuì*

   I may as well go. *Wŏ gān cuì qù.*

mean; base (morally low) *bēi bĭ*

   dirty tricks *bēi bĭ shŏu duàn*

   I mean it. *Zhēn de.*

I don't **mind**. *Bú zài hu.*

make a mistake *nòng cuò le*

   My mistake *wŏ cuò le*

Moon *yuè liang*

   The moon is very bright. *Yuè liang hĕn liàng.*

One **more**; another please. *Zài lái yí gè.*

It's your **move**. *Gāi ní zŏu; Gāi ní le.*

must have *yí dìng yào*

N

   given **name** *míng zi*

      What is his name? *Tā jiào shénme míng zi?*

      What is his surname? *Tā xìng shénme?*

      In name only (without substance). *Yŏu míng wú shí.*

nearby *fù jìn*
New Year *xīn nián*
    Happy New Year. *Xīn nián kuài lè.*
next time *xià yí cì*
Did you have a **nice time**? *Wán de hǎo ma?*
No; not the case *bú duì*
    don't want *bú yào*
    not need/require *bù xǔ yào*
    No need to thank me. *Bú yòng/bú bì xiè wǒ.*
    There is no more! *Méi yǒu le!*
    There is nobody. *Méi yǒu rén.*
    Not me. *Bú shì wǒ.*
    That's not so. *Bú duì.*
    not at home *bú zài (jiā)*
    not bad *bú huài*
    not so good *bù dà hǎo*
Just **now** *gāng cái*
    He came just now. *Tā gāng cái lái le.*

O

OK *xíng; ké yǐ*
    Is it OK? *xíng ma?; ké yǐ ma?*
    He's OK. *Tā rén bú cuò.*
    That's OK. *Xíng.*
    not OK *bù xíng*
Please **open** the door. *Qǐng kāi mén.*
    open, frank *tǎn bái de*
    open (not secret) *gōng kāi de*

opportunity (chance)   *jī huì*
> That's a good opportunity.   *Hǎo jī huì.*
> big opportunity   *dà jī huì*

ordinary   *píng cháng*
> out of the ordinary; special   *tè bié*

overdo it   *guò fèn*
> Don't overdo it.   *Bié guò fèn.*
> That's overdone it/over the top.   *Tài guò fèn.*

P

I have a **pain** in my stomach.   *Wǒ wèi téng.*

Pardon (polite apology).   *Dùi bù qǐ; qǐng yuán liàng.*

He's very **patient**.   *Tā hén yǒu nài xīn.*

perfect   *wán měi*
> It's perfect.   *Hǎo jí le.*

perhaps   *yé xǔ*

persuade   *shuō fú*
> I can't persuade him.   *Wǒ méi shuō fú tā*

place; location   *dì fang*
> out of place; not right   *bù xíng*

pleasant (of a person)   *hé qì*

Do as you **please**.   *(Qǐng) suí biàn.*

polite   *yóu lǐ mào*

practical (of things)   *shǐ yòng*
> practical (person)   *dǒng shì*

pray   *qí dǎo*
> I pray everyday.   *Wó měi tiān qí dǎo.*

pretty   *hǎo kàn*
> pretty (tune)   *hǎo tīng*

probably; be likely   *dà gài*
> He'll probably come.   *Tā dà gài lái.*

progress   *jìn bù*
pronunciation   *fā yīn*
> Good pronunciation.   *Fā yīn hén hǎo.*

proud   *jiāo ào*
a **publicity seeker**; show off   *tā hěn chū fēng tóu*
on **purpose**   *gù yì (de)*

Q

quality   *zhì liàng*
> good quality   *zhì liàng hén hǎo*

quantity   *shù liàng*
> a big quantity   *shù liàng hěn dà*

I have a **question**.   *Qǐng jiào yí xià.*
> without question; certainly   *yí dìng*

quick; fast   *kuài*
> Not so fast.   *Bié tài kuài.*

quiet; peaceful   *ān jìng*
> I like quiet.   *Wó xǐ huan ān jìng.*

Quit talking nonsense.   *Bié hú shuō.*
Quite so.   *Méi cuò.*

R

It never **rains** but it pours (lit. calamity not single happen).   *Huò bù dān xíng*

rather; comparatively   *bǐ jiào*
> That's rather good.   *Bǐ jiào hǎo.*

raw (not cooked) *shēng de*
  I like to eat it raw. *Wǒ ài chī shēng de.*
get **ready**; prepare *yù bèi*
Really? *Zhēn de ma?*
recently *zuì jìn*
regret *hòu huǐ*
  I don't **regret** it. *Wǒ bù hòu huǐ.*
I can't **remember**. *Xiǎng bù qǐ lái.*
represent(ative) *dài biǎo*
I **respect** him. *Wó hěn zūn jīng tā.*
responsible, trustworthy *kě kào; fù zé rèn*
You can **rest assured**. *Nǐ ké yǐ fàng xīn.*
restaurant *fàn guǎn*
The **results** were very satisfactory. *Jié guǒ hěn lìng rén
  mǎn yì.*
rich (money) *yǒu qián*
  abundant *fēng fù*
That's **right**! *Duì le!*
  right (politically); conservative *báo shǒu*
  Go right ahead, it's OK. *Ké yǐ.*
  Serves you right. *Huò gāi.*
All roads lead to Rome. *Tiáo tiáo dào dào tōng
  Luò Mǎ.*
rose (flower) *méi guì huā*
Round a corner (lit. and fig.) *guǎi wān*
  We've turned a corner (lit. and fig.) *Wǒ men yǐ jīng
    guǎi wān le.*
(As a **rule**) I don't drink. *Wǒ (xiàng lái) bù hē jiǔ.*
run a risk *mào xiǎn*
  It's risky. *Hěn mào xiǎn.*
What's your **rush**? *Nǐ máng shénme?*

S

It's a **sad situation**. *Zhēn kě lián.*

Safe; secure *ān quán*

Safety first. *Ān quán dì yī.*

Take with a grain of **salt** (not entirely believe). *Yóu diǎn huái yí.*

In the **same boat**. (lit. same illness mutual sympathy). *Tóng bìng xiāng lián*

The same to you. (in response to a compliment). *Bí cǐ bí cǐ*

be **satisfied** *mǎn yì*

say; speak *shuō*

Say it in English. *Yòng yīng wén shuō.*

What did you say? *Nǐ shuō shénme?*

speak *shūo*

I can't speak; words fail me *wǒ shūo bù chū laī*

Do I speak clearly enough? *Wǒ shuō de gòu qīng chu ma?*

heavily **seasoned** (food) *kǒu wèi tài zhòng*

give a **second** chance *yuán liàng yí cì*

keep a **secret** *bǎo mì*

I see (understand). *Míng bǎi le.*

sense of direction *fāng xiàng gǎn*

a **sense of humour** *yōu mò gǎn*

serious *yán sù*

sexy *xìng gǎn*

So that's how it is. *Yuán lái rú cǐ.*

short memory *jì xìng bù hǎo*

Show me how to do it. *Zuò géi wǒ kàn kàn.*

show off; a publicity seeker   *tā hěn chū fēng tóu*
Shut up!   *Bié (hú) shuō!*

Shut your mouth!   *Bì zuǐ!*

I'm going to be **sick**.   *Wǒ yào tù.*

be sick of, fed up   *tǎo yàn; nì fan*

simple, easy   *jiǎn dān*
simple minded   *shǎ*
sincere   *chéng shí*

He is not sincere.   *Tā bù chéng shí.*

May I **sit** down?   *Wǒ ké yǐ zuò xìa ma?*

The **sky** is cloudy.   *Yīn tiān le.*

I have a **slight cold**.   *Wǒ yóu diǎn gǎn mào.*

slow down   *màn yì diǎn*

sooner or later   *záo wǎn*

sorry   *duì bu qǐ*

feel sad; sorry   *nán guò*

I feel sorry (about that)   *wó hěn nán guò*

very **special**   *hěn tè bié*

spirit (disposition)   *jīng shén*

He's in high spirits.   *Tā fù yǒu jīng shen.*

strange; bizarre   *qí guài*

be a **stranger** (to something)   *bù xí guàn*

Congratulations on your **success**.   *Zhù hè nǐ de chéng gōng.*

suggestion   *jiàn yì*

Do you have a suggestion?   *Ní yǒu jiàn yì ma?*

That's a good suggestion.   *Hǎo jiàn yì.*

suitable   *hé shì*

not suitable   *bù hé shì*

suit yourself   *suí nǐ*

make **sure**/pay attention   *zhù yì*
Sure!   *Dāng rán; yí dìng!*
   Are you sure?   *Shì zhēn de ma?*
   I'm sure.   *Yí dìng.*

T

take a shot at/let me try   *ràng wǒ shì yí shì*
Take it easy.   *Bié zháo jí.*
Please **talk** more slowly.   *Qǐng shuō màn yì diǎn.*
   the talk of the town   *mǎn chéng fēng yǔ*
tasteful   *hén jiǎng jiu*
tasty   *hǎo chī*
Terrible, that's terrible, how unfortunate   *zhēn zāo gāo*
Thank you   *xiè xie*
   Thanks for going to the trouble.   *Má fan nǐ le.*
thing (indefinite material object)   *dōng xi*
   thing (event)   *shì*
I think so.   *Wó xiǎng shì*
touching (moving)   *gǎn dòng*
translate   *fān yì*
   Please translate it for me.   *Qíng géi wǒ fān yì.*
treasure   *bǎo bèi*
Treat all people as equals.   *Yí shì tóng rén.*
You've gone to a lot of **trouble**.   *Nǐ zhēn shì fèi xīn.*
True/false   *zhēn de/jiǎ de*
   Are you **telling the truth**?   *Nǐ shì shuō shí huà ma?*
   Is it true?   *Zhēn de ma?*

U

Uncommon; extraordinary   *bù píng fán*
understand   *dǒng*
> I understand; I see.   *Míng bǎi le.*
> I don't understand.   *Wǒ bù dǒng.*
> Do you get it; **understand**?   *Nǐ míng bǎi ma?*
> I don't understand very well   *wǒ tīng bú dà dǒng; bú tài dǒng*
> Do you understand?   *Dǒng le ma?*

It's so **unexpected**.   *Zhēn méi xiǎng dào.*
unrelated; no connection   *méi guān xi*
(not) very **useful**   *(méi) yǒu yòng*
> no use   *méi yòng*
> to be used to   *xí guàn*
> to be unused to   *bù xí guàn*

V

very   *fēi cháng*

W

Shall I **wait**?   *Wó děng zhe ma?*
Don't wash dirty linen in public.   *Jiā chǒu bù kě wài yáng.*
What   *shénme*
> **What** does that/this/it mean?   *Shénme yì si?*
> What else?   *Hái yǒu shénme?*

Where   *zài năr*
Who   s*huí*
Why   *weì shénme*
win-win   *shuāng yíng*
    win-win situation   *shuāng yíng jú miàn*
no **wonder**   *nán guài; guài bù dé*
wrong   *cuò le*

Y

yes; that's so   *duì le; shì*

22

An Introduction to the Chinese Writing System

It is desirable to have some knowledge of the Chinese writing system to understand both its relationship to the spoken language and also its significance as a cultural artifact in its own right. It also helps you to get around.

It is important to appreciate the difficulty in learning to write Chinese. Behind each sound is a unique written character with its own features and, in many cases, the weight of the literary language that gives rise to a multiplicity of meanings and associations. The spoken language without the script can only provide a monotone outline that while highly useful can in no way be considered to provide a complete picture of the object it represents.

Contemporary written Chinese includes words still that can be traced back to ancient prototypes from approximately 1300 BC. This early evidence of pictographic writing appears as carvings on animal bones and tortoise shell (only discovered in the 1920s) that were used for predicting the future. Today only a small proportion (some five per cent) of Chinese written characters (*wén zi*) are considered to be pictographic but all characters retain the same principles of discrete units of meaning that are determined by the systematic composition of the particular character.

Modern Chinese dictionaries generally have around 5000 individual monosyllabic character entries with words created by multiple combinations of this existing body of syllables. Words in Chinese are made by a combination of characters (usually two) and from a basic group of characters a large vocabulary can be derived. It has been observed that while the *Complete Works of Chairman Mao* contain some 900 000 characters, only just over 3000 different ones are commonly used. A knowledge of at least 2000 characters is considered necessary for a basic working knowledge of modern Chinese. The most complete dictionaries list over 50 000 entries and variants of individual characters that have developed over time.

Modern forms of characters have evolved according to several principles. For example, purely pictographic characters, such as sun (*ri* 日), moon (*yue* 月) and tree (*mu* 木) are still recognizable images of the objects they represent; ideographs depict more abstract concepts such as numbers (*yi er san* 一二三), above (*shang* 上), below (*xia* 下) and the word for 'good' (*hao* 好) which is represented by graphs for woman and child; the character 'bright' (*ming* 明) combines sun and moon.

Most characters (around eighty per cent) are in fact phonetically derived by combining graphs that indicate pronunciation as well as those more directly related to the meaning. These characters consist of a phonetic sound component along with a 'radical' element that classifies the meaning (e.g. wood, water, fire, speech, hand, heart etc.). There are 214 such radicals and most dictionaries are arranged in order of radical by the number of strokes used to write it, while the characters with the same radical are then ordered by the total number of strokes. It is worth noting, however, that modern dictionaries in China are increasingly being ordered by pinyin spelling according to the English alphabet.

Chinese characters are formed by eight basic stroke forms: dot, horizontal, vertical, left leaning, right leaning, hook, rising and cornering stroke. Complex radicals can have up to seventeen strokes. The simplification of characters, which has been progressively introduced in the People's Republic of China from the 1950s, is an attempt to address this particular complexity.

The order of the strokes is a critical part of learning Chinese characters and has particular consequences for the legibility of cursive script. Characters are written in accordance with a few basic principles: left to right, top to bottom, outside to inside and inside before closure. Each character fits into an imaginary square which on the page is separated by an equal space. Distinguishing the groups of syllables that form individual words presents challenges for the student reader (not unlike Latin before Julius Caesar introduced spaces between words). This cumbersome but orderly writing system, while requiring much rote learning, encourages modes of expression that are characterized by a terse vividness as well as a highly abstract conceptualization as many of the proverbial expressions introduced throughout the book illustrate.

Traditionally, China has valued the written over the spoken word. It is said that in imperial China it was considered improper to discard any printed matter so it had to be collected and burned with due ceremony. China's word for 'civilization' (*wén huà*) connotes the transforming power of the written word.

At a very early stage Chinese writing developed great aesthetic qualities, highlighting both linear and spatial relationships which are features that continue to distinguish all China's art forms. The balance and structural harmony of the composition of each character is the foundation of the highly prized art of calligraphy that sets great store by the mastery of the compositional relationships between the characters. Calligraphy unites form and expression in an infinite variety of expression of individual personality within the disciplines of the execution with brush and ink. Calligraphy expresses much of the central values of Chinese aesthetic sense and design whose appreciation reveals much about the Chinese cultural sensibility. The re-emergence of the traditional characters in daily use in China (e.g. on name cards, shop fronts and in the republication of older texts etc.) attests to an enduring appreciation of the inherent elegance and style of Chinese written script.

The following list of (simplified) characters are useful to recognize and provide a basic introduction to character forms.

Transport

行李	*xíng lǐ*	luggage
东	*dōng*	East
南	*nán*	South
西	*xī*	West
北	*běi*	North
火 车 站	*huǒ chē zhàn*	railway station
地 铁	*dì tiě*	underground (railway); metro

Out and about

男	*nán*	male
女	*nü*	female
禁 止	*jìn zhǐ*	prohibited
厕 所	*cè suǒ*	toilet
问讯处	*wèn xùn chù*	inquiries
公共	*gòng gōng*	public
不	*bù*	no
关	*guān*	closed
开	*kāi*	open
上	*shàng*	above/up
下	*xià*	below/under
拉	*lā*	pull
推	*tuī*	push
今日	*jīn rì*	today
出口	*chū kǒu*	exit
入 口	*rù kǒu*	entry

Numbers 1–10

一 二 三 四 五 六 七 八 九 十

外国人	*wài guó rén*	foreigner
太 平门	*tài píng mén*	emergency exit
出租	*chū zū*	for rent
请勿…	*qǐng wù…*	please do not….
楼 上	*lóu shàng*	upstairs
楼 下	*xià*	downstairs
小 心	*xiǎo xīn*	caution
满	*mǎn*	full
空	*kōng*	empty
自动	*zì dòng*	automatic
谢 谢	*xiè xiè*	thank you
内	*nèi*	inside
外	*wài*	outside
通 告	*tōng gào*	notice
洗 手 间	*xǐ shǒu jiān*	washroom (i.e. toilet)
公 司	*gōng sī*	company
左	*zuǒ*	left
右	*yòu*	right
共产党	*gòng chán dǎng*	Communist Party

Food

酒	*jiǔ*	wine/alcohol
咖 啡	*kā fēi*	coffee
茶	*chá*	tea
酱油	*jiàng yóu*	soy sauce
醋	*cù*	vinegar

Places

中国	*zhōng guó* China
寺	*sì* temple
天安 门	*Tiān ān mén*
长 城	*cháng chéng* Great Wall
北 京	*Běijīng*
上 海	*Shànghǎi*
广 州	*Guǎngzhōu*
故宫	*gù gōng* Forbidden City

Appendix A

Common Chinese surnames and forms of address

In this section you will find a selection of common surnames found in China. Needless to say, in many cases there are a number of ways in which the same sound can be written in Chinese script. There are ingenious ways of describing particular characters without the need to resort to writing them. Sounds that are also surnames are a useful method with which to practice pronunciation—particularly for the more uncommon sounds. Correct pronunciation of these sounds is also useful as you may end up with your given Chinese surname having one of the following sounds. It is a minor courtesy to pronounce the name of the person you are speaking with correctly, especially if it is your host.

The pronunciation of foreign surnames present significant challenges to non-speakers of English, and Chinese overcome this issue by conferring a Chinese name (formally or informally) on the foreign guest. Many foreign official visitors, as well as residents, find it expedient to have name cards that include a sinicized version of their name. It is common practice for the first syllable of the foreign surname to be translated with the closest approximation to the Chinese sound of a character generally used for a surname. The selection and explanation of the meaning of names can be a source of much entertainment.

Familiarity with the pronunciation of names also appreciates that there could often be occasions when it may be useful to recognize when your name (at least) is being referred to in conversation. The transliteration of foreign surnames is an instance of the Chinese penchant for practicality as well as a small example of the subtle assimilation of the foreign into the norms of Chinese culture. Names can also provide useful subjects for conversation in regards to their background and the circumstances of the selection of given names.

Today, traditional practices are being revived and propitious names can be selected with aid of classic texts like the *Book of Changes* (**Yi Jing**) used to divine fortune according to the number of strokes in the characters, among other features. You can always begin an interesting conversation by asking your dinner guests about their

Bái	Chén	Dīng	Duàn
Cài	Dēng	Dǒng	Fāng
Cáo	Diāo	Dù	Fèi

Gāo	Kāng	Pān	Xiāng
Gěng	Kē	Péi	Xiāo
Gòng	Kǒng	Qí	Xiè
Gǔ	Lǐ	Qiàn	Xú
Guān	Liáng	Qín	Yán
Guō	Lín	Qiū	Yáng
Hán	Liú	Róng	Yè
Hóu	Lú	Shī	Zhāng
Hú	Luó	Sòng	Zhào
Huà	Mǎ	Sū	Zhèng
Huáng	Máo	Sūn	Zhōu
Jī	Měng	Wáng	Zhū
Jiǎ	Mǐn	Wèi	Zhuāng
Jiǎng	Ní	Wú	
Jīn	Oū yáng	Xià	

names (once you have discussed the weather) before moving on to more serious matters!

The following is a selection of the more commonly encountered surnames.

In China, single character surnames number over 500. There are only rare instances of two syllable names being used for Chinese surnames. Some of these include include Sī Tú, Zhū Gé, Duān Mù and Gōng Sǔn.

Common titles and forms of address

The following words can be used *after* surnames (or as a substitute for a name).

xiān sheng   Mr

nǚ shì   Madam

zhǔ rèn   Director; Supervisor

xiáo jiě   Miss

sī zhǎng   Division Head

tài tai   Mrs (use with care)*

kē zhǎng   Section Head

fū ren   Madam (formal) wives of foreigners and other important people

zōng cǎi   Managing Director

cháng zhǎng   (factory) Director

fù cháng zhǎng   Deputy Director

jīng lǐ   manager

zǒng jīng lǐ   general manager

fù jīng lǐ   deputy manager

bù zhǎng   Minister (in government)

mù shī   Reverend (Protestant)

shén fu   Father (Catholic)

dà shǐ   Ambassador

lǎo shī   teacher/sir

jiào shòu   professor

guán zhǎng   Director (e.g. of a museum)

dǒng shì   Director (of the Board)

dǒng shì zhǎng   Chairman (of the Board)

---

*   now usually used in China to refer to a married foreign women. This word still has associations with the pre-1949 wealthy elite (i.e. as the mistress of a household). As a sign of the social changes occurring in China this usage is being revived.

Appendix B
Country names

The following selection of foreign countries and place names is a useful guide to the principles of transliteration into Chinese of foreign words. It is important to remember that just as foreign words are difficult to pronounce and remember for speakers of English, foreign words need to be sinicized to accommodate Chinese script as well as vocal patterns. Foreign personal names, as well as certain loan words, are assimilated into Chinese in a similar way, for example: *ā sī pī lín* (aspirin); *qiǎo kè lì* (chocolate); *xiāng bīn jiǔ* (champagne); *aò lín pǐ kè* (Olympic—the Games are referred to as *aò yùn*, an abbreviation of *aò lín pǐ kè yùn dòng huì*).

A particular nationality is created simply by adding the sound *rén* (person) to the relevant country (e.g. *Wǒ shi ā gēn tíng rén* I am an Argentinian).

Argentina   *ā gēn tíng*
Australia   *aò dà lì yà*

Austria   *aò dì lì*
Brazil   *bā xī*
Belgium   *bǐ lì shí*
Canada   *jiā ná dà*
Denmark   *dān mài*
Finland   *fēn lán*
France   *fǎ guó*
Germany   *dé guó*
Greece   *xī là*
India   *yìn dù*
Ireland   *ài ěr lán*
Italy   *yì dà lì*
Japan   *rì běn*
Hong Kong   *xiāng gǎng*
Korea (North)   *cháo xián*
Korea (South)   *hán guó*
Lebanon   *lì bā nèn*
Malaysia   *mǎ lái xī yà*
The Netherlands   *hé lán*
New Zealand   *xīn xī lán*
Norway   *nà wēi*
Pakistan   *bā jī sī tǎn*
The Philippines   *fēi lǜ bīn*
Russia   *è luò sī*
Singapore   *xīn jiā pō*
Spain   *xī bān yà*
Sweden   *ruì diǎn*
Switzerland   *ruì shì*
Taiwan   *tái wān*
Thailand   *tài guó*
The United Kingdom   *yīng guó*
The United States   *měi guó*

Bibliography

Beijing Foreign Languages Institute, Han Ying Ci Dian Compilation Committee 1978, *A Chinese-English Dictionary*, Commercial Press, Beijing.

De Barry, Wm Theodore et al. 1969, *Sources of Chinese Tradition*, vol. 1, Columbia University Press, New York.

Fenn, Courtenay H. 1948, *The Five Thousand Dictionary*, Harvard University Press, Cambridge, Mass.

Giles, Herbert A. 1912, *A Chinese-English Dictionary*, Shanghai

Hui Yu et al. 2006, *A New Century Chinese-English Dictionary*, Foreign Language Teaching and Research Press, Beijing.

Institute of Far Eastern Languages 1965, *Dictionary of Spoken Chinese*, Yale University Press, New Haven.

Kane, Daniel 2006, *The Chinese Language: Its history and current usage*, Tuttle Publishing, Singapore.

Leys, Simon 1997, *The Analects of Confucius*, WW Norton & Co., New York.

Lin, Yu Tang 1951, *The Importance of Living*, William Heinemann Ltd, London.

Mah, Adeline Yen 2002, *A Thousand Pieces of Gold: A memoir of China's past through its proverbs*, Harper Collins, London.

Mathews, R. H. 1969, *Mathew's Chinese-English Dictionary: Revised American edition*, Harvard University Press, Cambridge, Mass.

Mayers, William Frederick 1874, *The Chinese Readers' Manual*, Shanghai.

Reid, Daniel 2001, *The Tao of Health, Sex and Longevity: A modern practical approach to the ancient way*, Pocket Books, London.

Roberts, Moss 2001, *Laozi Dao de Jing: The book of the way*, University of California Press, Berkeley.

Rohsenow, John S. 2003, *ABC Dictionary of Chinese Proverbs*, University of Hawaii Press, Honolulu.

Smith, Arthur H. 1965, *Proverbs and Common Sayings from the Chinese*, Paragon Book Reprint Corp., New York.

Spence, Jonathan D. 1992, *Chinese Roundabout Essays in History and Culture*, W W Norton and Company, New York.

Wang, James J. 1994, *Outrageous Chinese: A guide to Chinese street language*, China Books and Periodicals Inc., San Francisco.

Williams, C.A.S. 2006, *Chinese Symbolism and Art Motifs*, 4th edn, Tuttle Publishing, Tokyo.

Yong He comp. 1998, *Easy Way to Learn Chinese Idioms (Chinese and English)*, New World Press, Beijing.